"Vern Poythress rescues the miracles of Jesus [...] means of his sanctified scholarship. As a pastor, [...] ing me make sense of the miracles for myself and in turn for my congregation."
Alistair Begg, Senior Pastor, Parkside Church, Chagrin Falls, Ohio

"Poythress serves as a sure-footed guide through the towering magnificence of Jesus's miracles, so that we readers can see them as the pulsing signs of redemption that they are—radiating his power and his lordship and, ultimately, the greatest work ever—the cross. The precision and tender pastoral practicality of *The Miracles of Jesus* will be sure to refresh every reader. Those who preach and teach will find the carefully layered depth of application a welcome help in unfolding the miracles to their people."
R. Kent Hughes, Professor of Practical Theology, Westminster Theological Seminary

"Because the miracles that marked the ministry of Jesus are the most significant in Scripture, this volume largely confines its attention to them and shows with rich insight how they are essential for revealing the full scope of the salvation he accomplished. Written with a broad audience in view and in the author's characteristically clear and winsome way, it will be read with great profit by those wanting to grow in understanding how the miracles of Jesus are essential for the gospel."
Richard B. Gaffin, Jr., Emeritus Professor of Biblical and Systematic Theology, Westminster Theological Seminary

"Blending profound insight with clear explanation, Vern Poythress shows us that Jesus's miracles are not merely random acts of kindness and power, but—most importantly—are signs pointing to the central events of his redemptive mission: his sacrificial death and mighty resurrection. Poythress leads us from the incarnation, healings, stilled seas, transfiguration, and other supernatural displays of Jesus's identity as glorious God, last Adam, and promised Messiah to the cross and empty tomb. Then he leads us on to the application in our own lives and struggles with sin and suffering. I highly recommend this reader-friendly and Christ-glorifying study."
Dennis E. Johnson, Professor of Practical Theology, Westminster Seminary California

"We all encounter both believers and unbelievers who firmly deny that miracles of any kind happen today. Then we meet other believers and unbelievers who claim to experience miracles at nearly every turn. Poythress speaks to both extremes in a way that strikes at the heart of the matter. Jesus of Nazareth was the greatest miracle-worker the world has ever seen. But why? His miracles bore witness to him as the Savior and to the good news of God's miraculous kingdom coming to earth as it is in heaven."

Richard L. Pratt Jr., President, Third Millennium Ministries

"Vern Poythress is a master of New Testament interpretation, whose scholarship has shaped a generation of preachers. *The Miracles of Jesus* is a treasure trove that will radically influence the reader's understanding of Jesus's miracles. Poythress shows that, beyond proving Jesus's divine authority, the miracles are actually powerful gospel displays of the wide scope our his saving work. If you wish to understand better how deep and wide is the redeeming love of Jesus, read this book and rejoice!"

Richard D. Phillips, Senior Minister, Second Presbyterian Church, Greenville, South Carolina

"I am delighted to see available the principles and particulars of interpreting miracle stories that shaped my own understanding as a student of Vern Poythress. In characteristic fashion, he develops profound principles in the most accessible terms and proceeds to demonstrate their application through numerous examples from Matthew's Gospel. I'm enthused to be able to put this book into the hands of my students."

Michael J. Glodo, Associate Professor of Practical Theology, Reformed Theological Seminary

The Miracles of Jesus

*How the Savior's Mighty Acts Serve
as Signs of Redemption*

Vern S. Poythress

WHEATON, ILLINOIS

Library of Congress Cataloging-in-Publication Data
Poythress, Vern S.
    The miracles of Jesus : how the Savior's mighty acts serve as signs of redemption / Vern S. Poythress.
      pages cm.
    Includes bibliographical references and index.
    ISBN 978-1-4335-4607-5 (trade paperback)
    ISBN 978-1-4335-4610-5 (e-Pub)
    ISBN 978-1-4335-4608-2 (PDF)
    1. Jesus Christ—Miracles. 2. Bible. New Testament—Criticism, interpretation, etc. I. Title.
BS2545.M5P65   2016
232.9'55—dc23   2015005318

Since this book is concerned for pastoral ministry
and for counseling, it is fitting to dedicate it
to my son Justin, gifted in pastoral ministry,
to my son Ransom, gifted in counseling,
and to my new daughter Lisbeth, gifted in counseling

Contents

Part IV
THE RESURRECTION OF CHRIST AND ITS APPLICATION

Illustrations

Part I

INTRODUCING MIRACLES

1

The Reality of the
Miracles of Jesus

In the Bible, the four Gospels—Matthew, Mark, Luke, and John—record miracles that Jesus worked when he was on the earth. He healed leprosy, blindness, and many other diseases. He multiplied five loaves and two fish. He cast out demons. He walked on water. He raised the dead.

Questions about Miracles

It is an extraordinary record, but it raises many questions. For many modern people, at the top of the list of questions is whether the miracles really took place. And then, if they did take place, what is their meaning? How did they happen? Why did they happen? Why did the Gospels record them? And what are we supposed to make of them? How are they relevant to us?

We want primarily to address the questions about the meaning and relevance of miracles. But it is also important to address the question of whether the miracles really happened. Miracles confront us with the question of what kind of world we live in. Does the nature of the world allow for miracles, or is the world closed to them? Is the world just a self-sufficient mechanism that allows no deviation from its regularities? Questions about the world quickly lead to questions about God. Does God exist? If he does exist, is he the *kind* of God who would work miracles? And why would he do so? Who is Jesus, the one through whom the miracles took place?

Did Jesus's Miracles Really Happen?

People have debated the reality of miracles for centuries. Whole books have been written. Since we are focusing on the *meaning* of miracles, we will not cover in detail the long-standing debates about the existence of miracles. For a thorough discussion of the debates, I would recommend two recent books, which include references to many earlier books: C. John Collins, *The God of Miracles*; and Craig Keener, *Miracles.*[1]

Rather than have a thorough discussion here, we content ourselves with a brief look at the main issues that arise about the reality of miracles.

The existence of God. The first issue concerns the existence of God. At the foundation of the debate lies the issue of whether God exists, and what kind of God he is. Miracles as the Bible describes them are not merely unusual events or events for which people have not yet found a scientific explanation. They are acts of God, which dramatically indicate his power at work. If God does not exist, clearly miracles also do not exist.

What kind of God. A second issue concerns what *kind* of God exists. Deism pictures God as a God who created everything but afterward is not involved in the day-to-day operation of the world. He is distant. In general, deists believe that God set up the world so that it is a perfect mechanism and needs no "intervention" from him. A miracle would be like admitting that the mechanism has a defect. Accordingly, most deists maintain that miracles do not occur.

---

[1] C. John Collins, *The God of Miracles: An Exegetical Examination of God's Action in the World* (Wheaton, IL: Crossway, 2000); Craig S. Keener, *Miracles: The Credibility of the New Testament Accounts* (Grand Rapids, MI: Baker, 2011). See also Vern S. Poythress, *In the Beginning Was the Word: Language—A God-Centered Approach* (Wheaton, IL: Crossway, 2009), chapter 29.

A modern materialistic worldview, influenced by science, believes that the world consists most basically in matter and motion, governed by inviolable mechanistic laws. Most materialists do not believe in the existence of God. But even if he exists, he is irrelevant to the day-to-day functioning of the world. His status is similar to that within deism.

So which is true? We may observe briefly that God, as he is described in the Bible, is a God who acts both to create the world initially and afterward to sustain the world that he has created. The Bible indicates not only that God's existence is displayed through the things he has made, but that he has made himself known to all human beings through what he has made. All people *know* God, but they suppress this knowledge and make themselves substitutes for the true God:

> For the wrath of God is revealed from heaven against all ungodliness and unrighteousness of men, who by their unrighteousness suppress the truth. For what can be known about God is plain to them, because God has shown it to them. For his invisible attributes, namely, his eternal power and divine nature, have been clearly perceived, ever since the creation of the world, in the things that have been made. So they are without excuse. For although they knew God, they did not honor him as God or give thanks to him, but they became futile in their thinking, and their foolish hearts were darkened. Claiming to be wise, they became fools, and exchanged the glory of the immortal God for images resembling mortal man and birds and animals and creeping things. (Rom. 1:18–23)

Arguments about the existence of God may be useful as a kind of tool for reminding people of what they already know. But the value of such arguments is limited because no one is religiously neutral. Human beings are in flight from God.

According to Scripture, God is continually active in the regularities of the world as well as in any unusual events. His governing word is the real source of what scientists call scientific law.[2] He is the King and Lord over both the regularities and the exceptions. The regularities in God's rule are what make science possible. Far from being in tension with science, God is the foundation for science.

In addition, God is a personal God, not a mechanical system. So he can also bring about exceptions to the regularities when he wishes. Miracles are not only possible but are understandable and natural, given the fact that at times God may have special purposes that lead to special actions. For example, Christ's resurrection from the dead was exceedingly unusual, but it makes sense when we understand that in this event God the Father vindicated Christ and rewarded him for his obedience. Through Christ he now brings salvation to those who are united with Christ. The resurrection of Christ makes sense within a world governed by God. It does not make sense if the world is governed by impersonal, mechanistic laws.

Credibility of the miracles in the Gospels. Third, we have the question of whether the testimony about miracles found in the Gospels is credible. Once again, whole books have been written on this. The testimony will never be credible to a modern person if he has already decided that God does not exist or that miracles are impossible. But if he believes that God exists and that miracles are possible, the issue still remains as to whether particular miracles actually took place. For example, what about Jesus's casting out demons (Matt. 8:28–34) or his healing the centurion's slave (Matt. 8:5–13)? Did these particular events really take place, and did they take place in the manner described in the Gospels?

There are three subquestions involved here. One is whether the human beings who wrote the Gospels intended to claim that the events really happened. Even a naive reading suggests that they did. And this naive impression is confirmed by an explicit statement in Luke 1:1–4 concerning Luke's historical investigation. He says

---

[2] Vern S. Poythress, *Redeeming Science: A God-Centered Approach* (Wheaton, IL: Crossway, 2006), especially chapter 1.

that he wrote his Gospel in order that "you may have certainty concerning the things you have been taught" (v. 4). The Gospel of John indicates that it has recorded "things that Jesus did" (21:25). It provides this record "so that you may believe that Jesus is the Christ, the Son of God, and that by believing you may have life in his name" (20:31). This purpose presupposes the claim that John is not just providing fiction.[3]

Second, were the writers of the Gospels actually successful? Are the Gospels historically reliable, at least as reliable as reports from other human historians? It is helpful to look at the book of Acts, which was written by the same human author as the Gospel of Luke (see Acts 1:1). Some of the information in Acts about the Roman Empire can be cross-checked using information about Rome from other sources, and this checking confirms the reliability of Acts. Modern defenses of reliability go into this kind of information.[4] Again, because of our focus, we will leave this discussion to other books.

Third, do the Gospels have not merely human authority but also divine authority in what they say? If so, then they are completely true and trustworthy in what they say about miracles. They are not just more or less reliable, as a human historical writing might be, but are thoroughly reliable, because of the trustworthiness of God. Once again, whole books are devoted to the question.[5] I believe that the Gospels are indeed God's words, not merely human words. In my discussion of the Gospels, I accept the divine authority of what they say.

Who is Jesus? What we think about the miracles in the Gospels also depends on what we think about Jesus. If Jesus is the

---

[3] See further in Vern S. Poythress, *Inerrancy and the Gospels: A God-Centered Approach to the Challenges of Harmonization* (Wheaton, IL: Crossway, 2012), chapters 5–6.
[4] See, for example, F. F. Bruce, *The New Testament Documents: Are They Reliable?* (Grand Rapids, MI: Eerdmans, 2003). We also have defenses that focus on the Gospels rather than on Acts: Craig Blomberg, *The Historical Reliability of the Gospels*, 2nd ed. (Downers Grove, IL: InterVarsity Press, 2007); Blomberg, *The Historical Reliability of John's Gospel: Issues and Commentary* (Downers Grove, IL: InterVarsity Press, 2002).
[5] John M. Frame, *The Doctrine of the Word of God* (Phillipsburg, NJ: Presbyterian & Reformed, 2010); N. B. Stonehouse and Paul Woolley, eds., *The Infallible Word: A Symposium by the Members of the Faculty of Westminster Theological Seminary* (Philadelphia: Presbyterian & Reformed, 1967).

Messiah, the Son of God, promised by Old Testament prophecies, the miracles make sense as a fitting accompaniment to his work. If, on the other hand, a person does not believe that Jesus is the Messiah, that person may also be skeptical about the reports of miracles. The issue of Jesus's identity may also have an influence on the earlier questions about God and about the nature of Scripture. If the Bible's view is correct, Jesus is the way to God (John 14:6), and beliefs about him may radically influence a person's belief in God. Because Jesus testifies to the divine authority of the Old Testament, a decision about Jesus also affects one's decision about the character of Scripture.

Searching for Truth

All of these questions about God, miracles, and the identity of Jesus are important. As we have observed, we can find whole books that discuss the issues. But in this book we focus instead on the meaning of the miracles. So we provide only very short answers to all the preliminary questions.

If a person is plagued by questions, I could say that he should consult books such as those that I have cited above in footnotes. But he might also begin simply by reading the four Gospels, again and again. As he reads, he asks who Jesus is. And, since there is always sinful human resistance to accepting who Jesus really is, and his claims on our lives, I recommend asking God to reveal what is the truth and to overcome our own resistance. A person uncertain about whether God exists can ask, "God, if you exist, please reveal the truth as I read."

Before they begin reading, some people might want to try to find out whether the Gospels are historically reliable, at least on the level of human writings. So they would read some of the books discussing the question of historical reliability. But it would also be possible to start with the Gospels themselves. A person may find, when reading, that Jesus makes claims on his life that he cannot evade. So the theoretical question of historical reliability, which otherwise a person might want to debate in a vacuum, turns out not to be as important as it initially appeared to be. Jesus is unique. There is no one like him, among the founders or leaders of other religions or even among the other persons mentioned in the Bible. What he said and did is unique. It is so striking—and so convicting—that a person may realize that no human being could have invented what is found in the Gospels.

If a person comes to see that Jesus is who he claims to be, many things follow. Our own lives have to change, because Jesus calls us to be his disciples. And when we become his disciples, we accept what he says. What he says about the Old Testament confirms its divine authorship and authority.[6] And then that same authority extends to the New Testament, which is an addition to the Old Testament, commissioned by Jesus himself.

The consequence is that the person who encounters Jesus and who travels down the route to becoming his disciple gets his fundamental questions answered. The Bible contains clear answers to his questions. The answers include the following:

- God exists. There is only one God.
- God created the world and continues to rule over it (in "providence").
- God can work miracles when he wishes.
- God does work miracles at times when miracles further his purposes.
- We know that the Gospels present trustworthy historical accounts, because the Gospels are writings not only with human authors but with God as their divine author. What they say is God's word.
- The miracles in the Gospels actually took place in time and space, in the way in which the Gospels describe them.
- Jesus is who the Gospels say he is. He is both God and man, and he became incarnate (took on human nature) in order to bring salvation and to fulfill the promises made in the Old

---

[6] John Murray, "The Attestation of Scripture," in Stonehouse and Woolley, *Infallible Word*, 20–28.

Testament concerning the coming of the Messiah in the line of David.

The Meaning of Miracles

Granted that the miracles in the Gospels really happened, what do they show? Why were they done? Why did God bring them about? Those are the questions on which we will focus.

2

The Significance of Miracles

If some atheists or agnostics were to concede that some of the extraordinary events in the Gospels actually happened, could they just say that "strange things happen"? Are the extraordinary works of Jesus just strange events, weird events that lie outside normal patterns, without any rationale? Or are they works of God that reveal his purposes? And if so, what purposes do they reveal?

The Gospels do not treat the miracles of Jesus as if they were weird or irrational events. They are certainly extraordinary, but they make good sense as indicators of the character of Jesus's ministry as a whole. The people who saw Jesus's miracles interpreted what happened. For example, when Jesus raised from the dead a widow's son in Nain, the people reacted in this way:

> Fear seized them all, and they glorified God, saying, "A great prophet has arisen among us!" and "God has visited his people!" (Luke 7:16)

There is some evidence that Nain may have been near to Old Testament Shunem, where Elisha restored to life the Shunammite's son (2 Kings 4:18–37). Elijah also raised a widow's dead boy to life, in Zarephath (1 Kings 17:17–24). The people saw that Jesus's miracle was analogous to those of the two Old Testament prophets. The miracles showed the power of God at work, and they attested to the authenticity of the prophet. So the people saw Jesus's miracle as a work of God: "God has visited his people!" And they saw Jesus as a prophet of God: "A great prophet has arisen among us!" The people did not yet realize that Jesus was God come in the flesh. But they did realize that God was at work through him.

Modern Relevance

The miracles of Jesus were relevant to the people back then. But what about now? The Gospels record the miracles in order to indicate what happened. But the Gospels also have a religious purpose. Through understanding who Jesus is and what he did, we are invited to place our faith in him. John is the most explicit about this purpose of miracles:

> Now Jesus did many other signs in the presence of the disciples, which are not written in this book; but these are written so that you may believe that Jesus is the Christ, the Son of God, and that by believing you may have life in his name. (John 20:30–31)

The Gospels indicate that Jesus lived on earth long ago, but now continues to live in heaven, having ascended to the right hand of God (Acts 2:33). The same Jesus who acted with power and compassion on earth still acts with power and compassion now. He acts to save people from their sins, restore them to fellowship with God, and give hope for a future resurrection from the dead. At the future time of resurrection, God's purposes for individuals and for the cosmos as a whole will be fully realized (Rom. 8:18–25).

Each of the miracles of Jesus happened uniquely at one time and at one place. In their detailed configuration they will never be repeated. But they have pertinence for us now, because they are "signs." The Gospel of John characteristically uses the word *sign* (Greek *semeion*) rather than other words like *miracle* and *wonder*. It thereby indicates that the miracles have permanent meaning.

They *signify* truths concerning God, concerning Christ, and concerning the salvation he has brought. John—and the other Gospels as well—urges us to listen. By taking to heart the significance of signs, we hear what God himself is saying to us; and by hearing we may be transformed, both now and in the future.

Three Kinds of Significance

The miracles of Jesus have at least three kinds of significance, corresponding roughly to three aspects of who Jesus is. (1) Jesus is God. (2) Jesus is fully human, and as a human being performed miracles in a way analogous to the miracles of Old Testament prophets. (3) Jesus is the Messiah promised in the Old Testament, the one mediator between God and man. (See fig. 2.1.)

Fig. 2.1: Significance of Jesus's Miracles

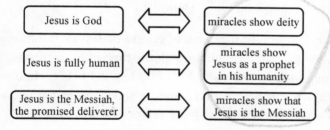

Let us begin with the first aspect, namely Jesus's deity. John 1:1 indicates that Jesus is God. From all eternity he exists as the Word, the second person of the Trinity. The miracles as works of divine power confirm his deity. In the minds of many Christian readers, Jesus's deity is what stands out in the miracles.

But the people who originally saw Jesus's miracles did not understand their full significance right away. We already observed that in Luke 7:16 the people identified Jesus as "a great prophet." He was indeed a prophet; but he was more. He was God come in the flesh (John 1:14).

Consider the miracles in the Old Testament that took place through prophets like Elijah and Elisha. These miracles were works of *divine* power. God brought them about. Elijah and Elisha did not accomplish them by their own innate power. Should we say exactly the same thing about Jesus? No, because Jesus made claims that went beyond those of Old Testament prophets. He is the unique Son of the Father, and his name is honored alongside the name of the Father and the Spirit as a divine name (Matt. 28:19). When we understand the miracles of Jesus in the context of who he is, we see that they are works that Jesus did by his own divine power, not merely works of God done through a human prophet:

> . . . the Son *gives life* to whom he will. (John 5:21)

> For this reason the Father loves me, because I lay down my life that I may *take it up again.* No one takes it from me, but I lay it down of my own accord. I have authority to lay it down, and I have authority to take it up again. (John 10:17–18)

A second kind of significance arises because of Jesus's full humanity (again, see fig. 2.1). Beginning with the time of his incarnation, Jesus is fully man as well as fully God (Heb. 2:14–18). He is one person with two natures, the divine nature and a human nature. This is a deep mystery. As a man, Jesus performed works similar to those of Old Testament prophets. This is true *in addition* to the truth that we just observed about Jesus doing works by his own divine power.

A third significance concerns Jesus's unique role as the Messiah, the great deliverer in the line of David who is prophesied in the Old Testament. For example, Isaiah 9:6–7 and 11:1–9 foretell the coming of the Messiah in the line of David. Isaiah 61:1–2 describes the servant of the Lord as one filled with the Holy Spirit in order to release captives. Jesus quoted from the passage in Isaiah 61 while in the synagogue at Nazareth, and indicated that it was fulfilled in him (Luke 4:18–21). When John the Baptist sent messengers to Jesus, Jesus pointed to his miraculous works as signs of fulfillment (Luke 7:22), against the background of Isaiah 35:5–6:

Then the eyes of the blind shall be opened,
>and the ears of the deaf unstopped,
then shall the lame man leap like a deer,
>and the tongue of the mute sing for joy.

Thus, Jesus's miracles fulfill Old Testament prophecy.

It is now almost two thousand years since Jesus accomplished his miracles. The people of God have had much time to reflect on his miracles. Much has been written that is profitable. But we may still add to it by noting ways in which each of the miracles functions as a small picture of Christ's glory and of his mission of salvation. The miracles tell stories that show analogues to the grand story of redemption. God redeems people from sin so that they may enter into the glory of God's presence. The small stories of redemption point especially to the climax of redemption in Christ's crucifixion, death, resurrection, ascension, reign, and second coming.[1]

These stories have pertinence to us because God's call to salvation still goes out to sinners today:

The times of ignorance God overlooked, but now he *commands all people everywhere* to repent, because he has fixed a day on which he will judge the world in righteousness by a man whom he has appointed; and of this he has given assurance to all by raising him from the dead. (Acts 17:30–31)

And there is salvation in no one else, for there is no other name under heaven given among men by which we must be saved. (Acts 4:12)

And let the one who is thirsty come; let the one who desires take the water of life without price. (Rev. 22:17)

In the twentieth century and the beginning of the twenty-first century, the appreciation for analogies among redemptive stories has faded somewhat among scholars, for various reasons. So it is

---

[1] See the discussion in Vern S. Poythress, *In the Beginning Was the Word: Language—A God-Centered Approach* (Wheaton, IL: Crossway, 2009), chapters 24–29

important to explore these analogies. Other books have laid theoretical groundwork to justify the process.[2] I have also found one
book by Richard Phillips that explains, in a pastoral way, the implications of Jesus's miracles for today by relying on redemptive
analogies.[3] In this present book I intend to show the nature of these
redemptive analogies. God has built redemptive analogies into history. It is these redemptive analogies, which lie *behind* Phillips's
book, that enable him to do such a good job in expounding the
significance of miracles. Phillips's book focuses on the miracles in
the Gospel of Luke. To complement his work, I will focus primarily
on the miracles in John and in Matthew.

---

[2] In particular, Vern S. Poythress, *God-Centered Biblical Interpretation* (Phillipsburg, NJ: Presbyterian
& Reformed, 1999); Poythress, *In the Beginning Was the Word*, chapters 24–29; Poythress, *Iner-
rancy and Worldview: Answering Modern Challenges to the Bible* (Wheaton, IL: Crossway, 2012);
Poythress, *Inerrancy and the Gospels: A God-Centered Approach to the Challenges of Harmoniza-
tion* (Wheaton, IL: Crossway, 2012); Poythress, *Reading the Word of God in the Presence of God:
A Handbook for Biblical Interpretation* (Wheaton, IL: Crossway, forthcoming).
[3] Richard D. Phillips, *Mighty to Save: Discovering God's Grace in the Miracles of Jesus* (Phillipsburg,
NJ: Presbyterian & Reformed, 2001).

Part II

MIRACLES AS SIGNS

3

Illustrative Miracles from
the Gospel of John

The Gospel of John discusses more explicitly how the miracles of Jesus are signs of redemption. So we may begin with several miracles recorded there.

The Bread of Life

Let us first look at John 6, which records the miracle of the feeding of the 5,000 (John 6:1–14). The same miracle is recorded in the three other Gospels (Matt. 14:13–21; Mark 6:30–44; Luke 9:10–17), but John alone includes later in the same chapter Jesus's discourse about the bread of life (John 6:25–59). This discourse took place on the day after the miracle (v. 22).

Jesus began his discussion by mentioning the miracle: "Truly, truly, I say to you, you are seeking me, not because you saw signs, but because *you ate your fill of the loaves*" (v. 26). He then continued the discussion in a way that makes clear the parallel between the physical food from the loaves and the spiritual food that gives eternal life: "Do not work for the food that perishes, but for the food that endures to eternal life, which the Son of Man will give to you" (v. 27). At one point the crowd mentioned the manna from heaven (v. 31). Jesus then picked up on the theme of manna and used it to direct them to the true bread from heaven:

> Jesus then said to them, "Truly, truly, I say to you, it was not Moses who gave you the bread from heaven, but my Father gives you the true bread from heaven. For the bread of God is he who comes down from heaven and gives life to the world." (vv. 32–33)

He then declared, "I am the bread of life" (v. 35).

Jesus thus indicated that both the manna from the time of Moses and the miracle of feeding the 5,000 have symbolic significance. The manna came in a miraculous way, but even its miraculous character did not make it a source of eternal life; it served only to sustain temporal life. Similarly, the bread that multiplied to feed the 5,000 men sustained physical life (vv. 26–27), but Jesus indicated that both point to something deeper, namely to eternal life. Jesus himself is the one who supplies eternal life. Eternal life belongs to those who "feed on" him: "Whoever feeds on my flesh and drinks my blood has eternal life, and I will raise him up on the last day" (v. 54).

Thus the miracle of the feeding of the 5,000 has a symbolic significance beyond the fact that it displays divine power. Its significance goes beyond confirming and testifying to the fact that Jesus is an authentic messenger of God, like one of the Old Testament prophets. The miracle shows in symbolic form what Jesus is doing spiritually through his life, death, and resurrection—he is bringing eternal life, and giving lasting spiritual nourishment to everyone who comes to him in faith. (See fig. 3.1.)

Fig. 3.1: Jesus as the Bread of Life (John 6)

Jesus provides bread for 5,000 ⟹ Jesus provides eternal life through his flesh

The Light of the World

Consider a second miracle, the healing of the man born blind, recorded in John 9. This miracle shows divine power. But it is also a *sign*. It signifies what kind of person Jesus is and what he has come to earth to do. Note that it follows chapter 8, where Jesus declared, "I am the light of the world. Whoever follows me will not walk in darkness, but will have the light of life" (John 8:12). Just before healing the blind man, Jesus made a similar declaration, "As long as I am in the world, I am the light of the world" (John 9:5). By the end of the chapter, Jesus has made it clear that physical healing is symbolic of spiritual healing from spiritual blindness:

> Jesus said, "For judgment I came into this world, that those who do not see may see, and those who see may become blind." Some of the Pharisees near him heard these things, and said to him, "Are we also blind?" Jesus said to them, "If you were blind, you would have no guilt; but now that you say, 'We see,' your guilt remains." (John 9:39–41)

The fundamental illumination consists in knowing the Father through the Son:

> Philip said to him, "Lord, show us the Father, and it is enough for us." Jesus said to him, "Have I been with you so long, and you still do not know me, Philip? Whoever has *seen* me has *seen* the Father. How can you say, 'Show us the Father'? Do you not believe that I am in the Father and the Father is in me? The words that I say to you I do not speak on my own authority, but the Father who dwells in me does his works. Believe me that I am in the Father and the Father is in me, or else believe on account of the works themselves." (John 14:8–11)

> And this is eternal life, that they *know* you the only true God, and Jesus Christ whom you have sent. (John 17:3)

> No one has ever seen God; the only God, who is at the Father's side, he has *made him known*. (John 1:18)

The physical miracle of healing the blind man went together with a spiritual work in the blind man, so that the man came to believe in the Son of Man (Jesus, the Messiah):

He said, "Lord, I *believe*," and he worshiped him. (John 9:38)

The blind man received spiritual sight, by which he believed in Jesus and was saved. Thus the physical miracle illumines the whole purpose of Jesus to redeem people and give them a saving knowledge of God. (See fig. 3.2.)

Fig. 3.2: Jesus as the Light (John 9)

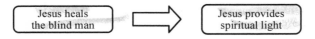

The Resurrection and the Life

The last miracle recorded in John as part of Jesus's public ministry is the resurrection of Lazarus (John 11:1–44). In the middle of the story, Jesus made a declaration about himself:

Jesus said to her, "I am the resurrection and the life. Whoever believes in me, though he die, yet shall he live, and everyone who lives and believes in me shall never die. Do you believe this?" (John 11:25–26)

Jesus here promised that believers will enjoy bodily resurrection: "though he die, yet shall he live." But bodily resurrection is the fitting accompaniment for the spiritual life that a believer *already* possesses: "everyone who lives and believes in me shall *never die.*" The *present* possession of eternal life is confirmed elsewhere in the Gospel of John:

Truly, truly, I say to you, whoever hears my word and believes him who sent me *has eternal life*. He does not come into judgment, but *has passed* from death to life. (John 5:24)

Whoever feeds on my flesh and drinks my blood *has eternal life*, and I will raise him up on the last day. (John 6:54)

And this is *eternal life*, that they know you the only true God, and Jesus Christ whom you have sent. (John 17:3)

What is the basis for this eternal life? It clearly comes from being united with Christ, who *is* the resurrection and the life. (See fig. 3.3.)

Fig. 3.3: Jesus as the Resurrection (John 11)

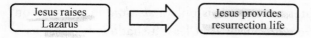

The Crucifixion and the Resurrection

As we observed, the raising of Lazarus is the last public miracle recorded in the Gospel of John—except for Jesus's resurrection. In response to the miracle with Lazarus, Caiaphas and the Jewish leaders took counsel together and plotted to kill Jesus, and to kill Lazarus as well (John 11:47–53; 12:10–11). The Gospel of John then continues with an account of Jesus's last days in Bethany and Jerusalem, culminating in his crucifixion and resurrection.

The whole account in the Gospel of John is leading up to the climax of Jesus's work in the crucifixion and the resurrection. Jesus himself described the importance of these coming events:

"Now is the judgment of this world; now will the ruler of this world be cast out. And I, when I am lifted up from the earth, will draw all people to myself." He said this to show by what kind of death he was going to die. (John 12:31–33)

The raising of Lazarus has a particularly close tie with Jesus's resurrection. It is a picture beforehand of his resurrection. But it is not on the same level as Jesus's resurrection. Lazarus, when brought back to life, was brought back to the *same kind* of life that he had before he died. He was still subject to meeting with death again in the future. Jesus, by contrast, has eternal life; he is never to die again (Rom. 6:9):

Christ has been raised from the dead, the firstfruits of those who have fallen asleep. (1 Cor. 15:20)

Christ is the "firstfruits." He is *not* the first human being ever to be restored to life. A restoration to life happened with the widow of Zarephath's son (1 Kings 17:17–24), with the Shunammite's son (2 Kings 4:18–37), and with Jairus's daughter (Matt. 9:18–26), as well as with Lazarus. So in what sense is Jesus first? Jesus in his humanity was the first to enter into the everlasting and unfailing life of the resurrection. The raising of Lazarus is thus a *type* or shadow of something greater to come. It is only a *shadow* in comparison with Jesus's resurrection. But it is at least a shadow. It offers us a small-scale picture of the eternal, spiritual life that Jesus will give as a result of his resurrection. (See fig. 3.4.)

Fig. 3.4: The Resurrection of Jesus

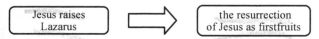

If the raising of Lazarus has a link forward to Jesus's resurrection, is the same true of other miracles in the Gospel of John? It is. Think of the feeding of the 5,000. This miracle depicts on a physical plane the reality that Jesus is the bread of life (John 6:35). Jesus went on in John 6 to explain that he offers nourishment by giving his own body and blood (vv. 53–56). These words point forward to Jesus's crucifixion and death, where he gave his body and blood as a sacrifice for sins. Spiritual nourishment takes place when we trust in Christ. By faith we are united with his crucifixion, death, and resurrection.

Jesus is always the bread of life. But the crucifixion and resurrection are the focal point of his work. Particularly in these climactic events he achieved what was necessary in order for the people of God to receive nourishment at all times.

Consider next Jesus's healing of the man blind from birth, and the associated claim, "I am the light of the world." John 1:4 indicates that even before his incarnation he was "the light" in a broad sense, by virtue of his role in creation: "In him was life, and the life was *the light of men*." In his incarnation he offered himself as the light of *redemption* in an intensive way:

> And the Word became flesh and dwelt among us, and we have seen his *glory*, glory as of the only Son from the Father, full of *grace* and truth. (John 1:14)

The light of revelation and of glory have their climax in the crucifixion and the resurrection, which reveal supremely the redemptive plan of God:

> Now is the Son of Man *glorified*, and God is *glorified* in him. If God is *glorified* in him, God will also *glorify* him in himself, and *glorify* him at once. (John 13:31–32)

> And now, Father, *glorify* me in your own presence with the *glory* that I had with you before the world existed. (John 17:5)

Thus, several miracles point forward to the great miracle of the resurrection of Christ. (See. fig. 3.5.)

Fig. 3.5: The Miracle of the Resurrection

The other miracles in the Gospel of John also point forward to the crucifixion and resurrection. We will consider them briefly, one by one.

The Man Sick for Thirty-Eight Years (John 5)

Let us consider the healing of the sick man at the Sheep Gate, in John 5. Jesus chose this occasion to give another discourse, John 5:19–47, which indicates the close relationship between the works of the Father and the works of the Son. The Son has healed the man as a "work" in which he is working the works of the Father (v. 17). The fact that Jesus performed the healing on the Sabbath day corresponds to the fact that God continues to work on the Sabbath day: "my Father is working until now" (v. 17). Jesus was thus inviting people to see his work of healing as a sign of his identity—he was performing the works of God, which the Father had given him to do. His works revealed his union with the Father: "the Father *who dwells in me* does his works" (14:10).

Moreover, an even greater work is coming:

> For the Father loves the Son and shows him all that he himself is doing. And greater works than these will he show him, so that you may marvel. For as the Father raises the dead and gives them life, so also the Son *gives life* to whom he will. (John 5:20–21)

The raising of dead human beings is based on Jesus's resurrection. So the earlier works that Jesus has done point to this greater work.

Jesus's works of healing address the various kinds of physical consequences that exist in an imperfect world, a world affected by the fall. In this world, human beings get sick. And sickness is a forerunner for death, the complete destruction of the functions of the body. The restoration of a man from sickness thus points to the greater restoration, the restoration of full bodily health in a resurrection body. And the foundation for this fuller restoration lies in Christ's resurrection. Healing is also a kind of metaphor for healing from sin. Christ forgives our sins; through the Holy Spirit he gives us the power to live new lives that are free from the dominion of sin (Rom. 6:7, 14).

Moreover, the freedom that we now have is a foretaste of the complete freedom from all sin that we will have in the new heaven and the new earth. We will be perfect in holiness, and also perfect forever in our new bodies. The healing of the sick man in John 5 functions to foreshadow this perfection, which Christ will bring us by virtue of his resurrection.

The Theme of New Creation

The healing in John 5 is part of a larger pattern of *new creation*. Jesus's ministry was a ministry of the kingdom of God that brought about new creation:

> Therefore, if anyone is in Christ, he is a new creation. The old has passed away; behold, the new has come. (2 Cor. 5:17)

In its final form, new creation includes the new heaven and new earth in Revelation 21:1. But new creation also has preliminary anticipations. Eternal life with Christ begins within our time period, because new spiritual life comes to individuals who are united to Christ. New life begins now, and comes to completion later. We say that it is *inaugurated* now, and *consummated* in the new heaven and new earth. We who belong to Christ are adopted as sons of God now (Rom. 8:15–17; Gal. 4:5–7; Eph. 1:5). This adoption comes to full realization in the future, at the time when creation is renewed (Rom. 8:23).

In the light of this relationship between inaugurated life and consummated life, we can see many signs of new creation in the New Testament. Being born again as described in John 3 is a kind of new creation. It represents the *inaugurated* stage of new creation. The resurrection of Lazarus is an anticipation of the final resurrection of the body, and this final resurrection is part of the larger picture of the creation of a new heaven and a new earth (Rev. 21:1). The resurrection of the body is the *consummated* form of new creation.

The word *eschatology* is a label for biblical teaching concerning the last things. In a narrow sense, *eschatology* has to do with teaching about the second coming of Christ, the last judgment, and the new heaven and new earth. But it can be used more broadly to label any events that belong to the fulfillment of Old Testament prophecies about "the last days." The coming of the kingdom of God during Jesus's earthly ministry is the beginning of that fulfillment, so it too belongs to eschatology. It is *inaugurated* eschatology, while the new heaven and new earth and the resurrection of the body belong to *consummated* eschatology.

We can see the pattern of inaugurated eschatology in John 9, with the man born blind. He received spiritual sight when he came to have faith in Jesus. That spiritual sight was an inaugurated form of spiritual sight. It anticipated the final form of sight, when God's servants will "see his face" (Rev. 22:4). They will see the glory of God in a fuller way than what is true today (Rev. 21:23; 22:5).

We can see the same pattern of inaugurated and consummated new creation with the miracle of feeding the 5,000. The miracle depicts the way in which Jesus is the bread of life to those who believe in him. But the food that we have from him now is also an anticipation of the consummation of being fed fully: we look forward to the marriage supper of the Lamb (Rev. 19:9).

Water into Wine

Consider next the miracle of water turned into wine. This miracle is also a "sign":

> This, the first of his *signs*, Jesus did at Cana in Galilee, and manifested his glory. And his disciples believed in him. (John 2:11)

So in what way is this miracle a "sign"? The meaning of this miracle is less obvious than with the miracles that we have already considered. But there are hints. The final verse, verse 11, says that Jesus "manifested his *glory*." The word *glory* has connections with the later discussion in John, concerning the way in which the glory of the Father and of the Son are shown through the events of the crucifixion and resurrection (John 13:31–32). Earlier in the story, Jesus said to his mother, "My hour has not yet come" (2:4). It sounds as if Jesus was giving a refusal to his mother. But then he did answer his mother's concern. The saying about "my hour" is cryptic. But it becomes clearer in the course of the Gospel of John that the "hour" in question is preeminently the time of his crucifixion and resurrection:

And Jesus answered them, "*The hour* has come for the Son of Man to be glorified" (John 12:23).

"Now is my soul troubled. And what shall I say? 'Father, save me from *this hour*'? But for this purpose I have come to *this hour*. Father, glorify your name." Then a voice came from heaven: "I have glorified it, and I will glorify it again." (John 12:27–28)

Now before the Feast of the Passover, when Jesus knew that *his hour* had come to depart out of this world to the Father, having loved his own who were in the world, he loved them to the end. (John 13:1)

When Jesus had spoken these words, he lifted up his eyes to heaven, and said, "Father, *the hour* has come; glorify your Son that the Son may glorify you, . . . (John 17:1)

In effect, Jesus was saying in John 2 that, though his "hour" was not yet at hand during the wedding at Cana in Galilee, it *would* eventually be at hand. And when it is at hand, it will become appropriate to ask him to provide wine for the feast—the feast of the kingdom of God. This feast fulfills the Jewish festivals, as well as the eschatological promise in Isaiah 25:6:

> On this mountain the LORD of hosts will make for all peoples
> a feast of rich food, a feast of well-aged *wine*,
> of rich food full of marrow, of aged *wine* well refined.

The wine is, in fact, his blood given to us to drink (John 6:53–56). The provision of physical wine for the wedding anticipates and foreshadows this greater festive provision, which Jesus accomplished in his crucifixion and resurrection.

This tie between the wedding miracle at Cana and the crucifixion and resurrection is reinforced by another, more subtle connection. Before the water became wine, it was water contained in "six stone water jars there for the Jewish rites of purification" (John 2:6). The water has a symbolic association with the Jewish rites of purification, which belong to the Old Testament. These rites have to do with *symbolic* purification, which is a type of the *real* purification that God will bring in eschatological salvation. The symbolism in the miracle at Cana includes a symbolic representation of the transition from the Old Testament level of types and shadows to the New Testament level of fulfillment. And how is fulfillment accomplished? Through Christ the Messiah. Just as Christ changed the water into wine, so he changed the entire course of history from one era to another. The "water" of shadows in the Old Testament became the "wine" of fulfillment in the New Testament.

The preceding chapter in John (chapter 1) contains an account of the ministry of John the Baptist, and this account is also relevant. John baptized with water. The water signified purification. But it was only a sign. John observed that it pointed to something greater that was going to follow him:

> John answered them, "I baptize with water, but among you stands one you do not know, even he who comes after me, the strap of whose sandal I am not worthy to untie." (John 1:26–27)

The one coming after John, that is, Jesus, is the one "who baptizes with the Holy Spirit" (John 1:33).

John the Baptist represents the terminus of the whole Old Testament order. He stood on the brink of the dawning of the eschatological kingdom of God, which came in Jesus. But what John did had to be superseded by what Jesus would bring. The miracle at Cana in Galilee symbolically signifies this transition, pointing backward to John as the last of the Old Testament prophets, and forward to the feast of the kingdom of God. This feast takes place by miraculously transfiguring the old, not by straight-line continuation of or addition to the old.

The miracle of water into wine has significance both for inaugurated eschatology and for consummated eschatology. The provision of eschatological wine by Jesus began with his "hour," the hour of his crucifixion and resurrection. The wine is his blood, through which we have eternal life even during the present age. This provision of wine is a form of inaugurated eschatology. At the same time, we look forward to the final form of eternal life in the new heaven and new earth, and the final marriage feast, namely the marriage supper of the Lamb (Rev. 19:9). This final feast is consummated eschatology.

Healing the Official's Son and Walking on Water

There remain two more miracles in the Gospel of John, about which less is said. One is the healing of the official's son, in John 4:46–54. John explicitly says that it is a sign and links it with the sign at Cana:

> So he came again to Cana in Galilee, *where he had made the water wine.* (John 4:46)

> This was now *the second sign* that Jesus did when he had come from Judea to Galilee. (v. 54)

The official's son was healed after being at the point of death. This healing from *near death* clearly foreshadows the complete victory over death that Jesus achieved. When he was crucified, Jesus actually died; he was not merely near death.

As usual, the significance of the miracle of healing the official's son includes both inaugurated eschatology and consummated eschatology. Inaugurated eschatology came when Jesus was raised from the dead; consummated eschatology will come when those who follow Jesus are raised, with resurrection bodies no longer subject to death.

We also have the miracle of Jesus walking on water, in John 6:16–21. It is closely connected with the miracle of the feeding of the 5,000, so John does not provide a separate commentary. At first glance Jesus's discourse on the bread of life in John 6:25–65 seems to have connections only with the feeding of the 5,000. But Jesus talked about having eternal life through communion with him. Jesus rescues people from eternal death, and large bodies of water can become symbolic of death, since a person can drown in them, and since sinking into the water is akin to "sinking" into the underworld of the grave. Thus Jonah's three days below the surface of the sea become a fitting symbol for death and resurrection:

> For just as Jonah was three days and three nights in the belly of the great fish, so will the Son of Man be three days and three nights in the heart of the earth. (Matt. 12:40)

Jesus's walking on water is a fitting symbol not only for mastery over nature but also for mastery over death. In this way it prefigures his resurrection. His resurrection constitutes inaugurated eschatology. He also provides new life for us, through his Spirit. Consummated eschatology comes with the resurrection of the bodies of believers.

Summary

Thus, each of the miracles in the Gospel of John foreshadows and points forward to the great miracle of Christ's resurrection. (See fig. 3.6.)

Fig. 3.6: Miracles Pointing to the Resurrection

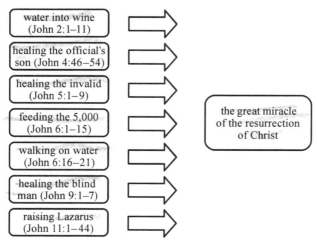

4

The Pattern of Redemption

Why do the miracles in the Gospel of John show a pattern in which they function like small pictures, foreshadowing the climactic redemption in Christ's crucifixion and resurrection? Are these connections with the crucifixion and resurrection something exceptional or strange? Or will we find similar connections in the other Gospels?

There are at least four main reasons why the connections are not exceptional, but belong to the very character of Jesus's ministry.

The Goal of Jesus's Ministry

First, Jesus's ministry has a unified character and a unified goal. Jesus understood himself as the Son sent by the Father to accomplish the Father's plan of redemption. He expressed his goal in a variety of ways:

> . . . even as the Son of Man came not to be served but to serve, and to give his life as a ransom for many. (Matt. 20:28)

> The Spirit of the Lord is upon me,
>   because he has anointed me
>   to proclaim good news to the poor.
> He has sent me to proclaim liberty to the captives

and recovering of sight to the blind,
    to set at liberty those who are oppressed,
to proclaim the year of the Lord's favor. (Luke 4:18–19)

For the Son of Man came to seek and to save the lost. (Luke 19:10)

For whatever the Father does, that the Son does likewise. (John 5:19)

These descriptions show the inner unity between Jesus's public ministry and his crucifixion and resurrection. Jesus's whole life on earth was a life in which he "served." But his service came to a climax when he gave "his life as a ransom for many." The release of captives, as described in Luke 4:18–19 in Jesus's quotation from Isaiah 61:1–2, took place all during his public ministry as he healed the sick and cast out demons. It came to a climax with the release from sin and death that he accomplished through his crucifixion and resurrection. In Jesus's public ministry he invited people to repent, and he had fellowship with notorious "sinners" like the tax collectors. He came to save the lost (Luke 19:10; cf. Matt. 9:12–13). Salvation for the lost took climactic form in his death and resurrection.

The Unity of the Kingdom of God

Second, the inner unity in Jesus's ministry and death is underscored with the expression "the kingdom of God." Jesus announced the coming of the kingdom of God (Matt. 4:17; Mark 1:15) and he embodied it in his ministry.

The expression "the kingdom of God" that Jesus used does not refer primarily to God's providential rule over all history, but to the exercise of God's *saving* power in climactic form. Jesus's ministry fulfilled Old Testament prophecies that looked forward to a final day when God would come and save his people. Jesus, as the messianic king and as God himself, manifested the saving rule of God during his life, and then climactically in his resurrection. Both his earlier ministry and his crucifixion and resurrection are aspects of a unified work of God, accomplishing the salvation promised in the Old Testament.

The Narrative Form of the Gospels, Leading to Climax

Third, each Gospel—each of the Synoptic Gospels as well as John—gives us a narrative account that leads somewhere. Each builds toward the crucifixion and resurrection as the climax of its narrative. We see Jesus introduced by John the Baptist, and then engaging in public ministry. The ministry was going somewhere: going to the cross. This goal is particularly highlighted when Jesus explicitly predicts his coming death, as in Matthew 16:21–23; 17:22–23; 20:17–19; 21:39; 26:2, and parallels in the other Gospels. Luke highlights the coming of the crucifixion by indicating already in Luke 9:51 that Jesus was going to Jerusalem (building on 9:31). The Gospels also show us the gradual intensifying opposition from the Jewish leaders, which points toward a final confrontation.

These ties between the middle of the story and its end invite us to see relationships between the individual episodes in Jesus's life and the goal to which these episodes are heading. The connections are all the more important because all the Gospels presuppose that God rules history. The incidents they record are not merely random but are divinely designed to work out God's purposes.

The Theological Unity of Redemption

Fourth, the Bible teaches that God's work of redemption—throughout history—has an inner unity. There is only one way of redemption, and that is through Christ and his work:

> Jesus said to him, "I am the way, and the truth, and the life. No one comes to the Father except through me." (John 14:6)

> And there is salvation in no one else, for there is no other name under heaven given among men by which we must be saved. (Acts 4:12)

> For there is one God, and there is one mediator between God and
> men, the man Christ Jesus, who gave himself as a ransom for all,
> which is the testimony given at the proper time. (1 Tim. 2:5–6)

All the smaller steps that bring blessing and deliverance and
restoration and health to people proceed from the grace of God,
which always comes ultimately on the basis of the work of Christ.
We do not deserve any of it. Because of sin, we deserve only death
(Rom. 6:23). It is Christ's work of substitution and victory that has
made it possible for God to "be just and the justifier of the one who
has faith in Jesus" (Rom. 3:26). The giving of wine at the wedding
in Cana, the healing of the official's son, and the healing of the sick
man at the Sheep Gate all manifested the grace of God to people
who did not deserve it. In their temporal order, these miracles pre-
ceded the death and resurrection of Christ. But in substance, they
depended on the grace made possible through Christ. Theologically,
there is a deep unity in all acts of grace, because they all have the
same basis in Christ.

We can see illustrations of this unity by thinking of redemptive
plots. All the miracles in the Gospels involve a transition from a situation of trouble or suffering to a situation of restoration or peace or
harmony, through an act of deliverance by Christ. This movement
from trouble to resolution is a simple plot structure, common to all of
the miracles. It is one factor that makes all of the miracles foreshadow
the crucifixion and resurrection. Christ's crucifixion and death involved Christ as our representative experiencing the deepest possible
difficulty. The resurrection resolved the difficulty. Because Christ
acted as our representative, this victory over difficulty also then gets
applied to us in the present age. But it was also applied beforehand,
as it were retroactively, to those to whom Christ ministered in his
earthly ministry, and to Old Testament recipients of grace as well.

Often the miracles in the Gospels show vivid foreshadowings of
the crucifixion and resurrection, at least with regard to some aspects
of the meaning of Christ's work. The vividness increases when the
particular *kind* of trouble already has an obvious symbolic relation-

ship to the deepest troubles of all—sin and death. For example, the raising of Lazarus is an answer to death, and so it has a vivid connection with the resurrection of Christ, which is the final answer to death. The healing of the man born blind has a vivid connection with healing of spiritual blindness and the giving of spiritual sight, because Christ has already announced that he is the light of the world (John 8:12). And this announcement has still further connections with the theme of spiritual light in the Gospel of John and in the Old Testament.

But in the broader sense, any healing from physical disease is pertinent. The plot of healing moves from sickness to health through Christ's work. The plot of redemption moves from the spiritual sickness of sin to the spiritual health of righteousness, and from the Adamic body doomed to die to the new spiritual body free from death (1 Cor. 15:44–49). Righteousness and freedom from death come through Christ's work.

The redemption that Christ accomplished is comprehensive in its implications. Christ was raised, as we observed, to imperishable life, the life characterizing the new heaven and the new earth (Rev. 21:4). In his experience he is the representative for the entirety of the new humanity. His resurrection results in the resurrection of the new humanity in due time (1 Cor. 15:22–26, 50–57). Not only so, but it is the basis for the comprehensive renewal of heaven and earth as well (Rom. 8:20–23; Rev. 21:1). So the movement from death to resurrection in the case of Christ's personal history is organically related to the movement from a broken to a restored and harmonious endpoint in every sphere of life.

Richard Phillips captures how the miracles of Jesus point to the climactic work of Jesus in his crucifixion and resurrection:

> In our study of the miracles of Jesus Christ we are working from the premise that we have before us something more than random acts of kindness. These miracles are not merely illustrations of Christ's goodness and power but are living sermons regarding the nature and purpose of his saving work.[1]

---

[1] Richard D. Phillips, *Mighty to Save: Discovering God's Grace in the Miracles of Jesus* (Phillipsburg, NJ: Presbyterian & Reformed, 2001), 21.

5

The Pattern of Application
of Redemption

Now let us consider how the miracles recorded in the Gospels have a bearing on people's lives today. To understand the connection of the Gospels to today, it is best first to step back and consider the very nature of redemption, according to the plan of God.

Redemption Accomplished and Applied

Theologians distinguish between the *accomplishment* of redemption and its *application*.[1] The accomplishment of redemption includes all the events of the incarnation, life, death, and resurrection of Christ. Christ *accomplished* redemption through his work. The *application* of redemption describes the work of Christ through the Holy Spirit in turning individuals from darkness to light, from the power of Satan to God (Acts 26:18), so that they are united to Christ in a life-giving way. They begin to live for God rather than for themselves. It also includes the work of God in the church as a corporate body (1 Corinthians 12). This application extends to today. People today are receiving eternal life through faith in

---

[1] John Murray, *Redemption Accomplished and Applied* (Grand Rapids, MI: Eerdmans, 1955).

Christ. They receive life through the Holy Spirit, who unites them to Christ.

The application of redemption includes the whole life of each Christian believer on earth, viewed from the perspective of what God does in his or her life: "For we are his workmanship, created in Christ Jesus for good works, which God prepared beforehand, that we should walk in them" (Eph. 2:10). The application of redemption also includes the works of God in believers subsequent to bodily death. They continue to be united to Christ and to live in his presence, awaiting the resurrection of the dead (Phil. 1:21, 23). At the last day, God raises believers from the dead and gives them transfigured, immortal bodies (1 Cor. 15:50–57). This bodily resurrection of individuals goes together with the renewal of creation and the appearance of the church in glorious form as the bride of Christ (Rev. 19:7–9; 21:2, 9).

The accomplishment of redemption and its application go together. They are like two sides of the same coin. When Christ accomplished redemption, he accomplished it in order that people might actually be saved. That is to say, accomplishment implies application. In the end, accomplishment of salvation does no good unless it comes to be applied to someone. Even the very concept of salvation implies that someone is going to be saved. Salvation has to come to people who are lost, and when it is applied to them they are no longer lost.

Conversely, the application of redemption presupposes its accomplishment. People can experience salvation only if God has already provided a basis for overcoming the enmity and guilt that belong to our fallen, sinful condition. The basis for overcoming our condition is the actual accomplishment of salvation. As we observed already, this basis was already being presupposed when people received the application of redemption during the Old Testament period. During that period, in a mysterious way, God applied beforehand to the saints the achievement of Christ. That achievement was yet to be accomplished in history, at the appropriate time (Gal. 4:4; 1 Tim. 2:6; 2 Tim. 1:10), but it was already certain according to the plan of God.

Union with Christ

The accomplishment and application of redemption belong together still more closely because of the way in which they come together in the biblical teaching about *union with Christ*. The Bible indicates that whatever blessings come to us in salvation come to us "in Christ":

> Blessed be the God and Father of our Lord Jesus Christ, who has blessed us *in Christ* with every spiritual blessing in the heavenly places, . . . (Eph. 1:3)

Christ is not only the *source* of blessings; he is the representative human being whose work and victory are reflected in those whom he represents. Christ died and was raised. We who trust in Christ have died and been raised *with him*:

> If *with Christ* you died to the elemental spirits of the world, . . . (Col. 2:20)

> If then you have been raised *with Christ*, seek the things that are above, where Christ is, seated at the right hand of God. (Col. 3:1)

> [God] raised us up *with him* and seated us *with him* in the heavenly places *in Christ Jesus*, . . . (Eph. 2:6)

The application of redemption includes the application of the pattern of Christ's death and resurrection to each believer.

Forms of the Application of Christ's Work to Us

The pattern of death and resurrection starts with Christ himself, who is our representative. The pattern is actually applied to us at the time of conversion and baptism:

> Do you not know that all of us who have been *baptized* into Christ Jesus were baptized into his death? We were buried therefore with him by baptism into death, in order that, just as Christ

was raised from the dead by the glory of the Father, we too might walk in newness of life. (Rom. 6:3–4)

Romans 6 proceeds to lay out the further implications of the application of the pattern of death and resurrection to us:

> For if we have been united with him in a death like his, we shall certainly be united with him in a resurrection like his. We know that our old self was crucified with him in order that the body of sin might be brought to nothing, so that we would no longer be enslaved to sin. For one who has died has been set free from sin. Now if we have died with Christ, we believe that we will also live with him. We know that Christ, being raised from the dead, will never die again; death no longer has dominion over him. For the death he died he died to sin, once for all, but the life he lives he lives to God. So you also must consider yourselves dead to sin and alive to God in Christ Jesus.
>
> Let not sin therefore reign in your mortal body, to make you obey its passions. (Rom. 6:5–12)

The pattern of Christ's life is applied to us in a decisive way at the beginning of the Christian life, so that the new life is indeed new. We have died to the old way of living, and we live now by the power of Christ's resurrection. But the Bible also indicates that the pattern of life, death, and resurrection is applied not only once and for all at the beginning, but daily:

> We are afflicted in every way, but not crushed; perplexed, but not driven to despair; persecuted, but not forsaken; struck down, but not destroyed; always carrying in the body the death of Jesus, so that the life of Jesus may also be manifested in our bodies. For we who live are always being given over to death for Jesus' sake, so that the life of Jesus also may be manifested in our mortal flesh. So death is at work in us, but life in you. (2 Cor. 4:8–12)
>
> . . . that I may know him and the power of his resurrection, and may share his sufferings, becoming like him in his death, that

by any means possible I may attain the resurrection from the dead. (Phil. 3:10–11)

The final application of this pattern of death and life comes at the time of bodily resurrection:

So is it with the resurrection of the dead. What is sown is perishable; what is raised is imperishable. . . . Just as we have borne the image of the man of dust [Adam], we shall also bear the image of the man of heaven. (1 Cor. 15:42, 49)

Thus there are several instances of the same pattern, all of which originate with Christ's death and resurrection:

1. Christ's death and resurrection, once and for all in history.
2. The believer's spiritual death and resurrection, at the beginning of the Christian life, as signified by baptism.
3. The believer's daily walk with Christ, which involves the experience of death and resurrection in union with him.
4. The final resurrection of the body.

All of these aspects of salvation serve to display the glory of God, and result in praise being given to him (Rom. 11:33–36; 1 Cor. 10:31; Rev. 4:11; 19:6–7). The different aspects of salvation take place for the benefit of the people who are saved. But the benefit to us is not the sole purpose, or even the main purpose, for the events. If it were, it would imply that God and Christ exist only to serve man. That is the exact reverse of the truth. We are created by God to serve and honor him. We are created in such a way that we find our highest joy in serving and honoring him. Our service is indeed a wonderful, spectacular benefit to us, but preeminently it serves the glory and praise of God.

The Connections with the Miracles in the Gospels

Now we may consider how the miracles in the Gospels have an organic connection to us. The miracles depict Christ's redemption. They foreshadow his work in the crucifixion and resurrection, just as Old Testament types foreshadow the work of Christ. They not only *depict* redemption; in some respects they also *embody* it. People with whom Christ interacted were "redeemed" in a sense—at least from sickness or demon possession or death. Some of them, like the man born blind, came to have saving faith in Christ (John 9:38). About others we are less certain. Many had some kind of belief about Jesus: they believed that Jesus was at least a prophet or a miracle worker, and that he had power to heal them. Jesus honored their belief. Was this belief a form of saving faith or not?

In some cases their belief may already have been a form of saving faith. It would have been like the saving faith that existed among the saints in the Old Testament. It would have been the first step to a more fully informed faith, a faith that included the conviction that Jesus was the Messiah and Savior of the world (John 4:42). But James reminds us that not everything that people call "faith" is necessarily saving faith (James 2:18–20). Only God knows all hearts. Faith for physical healing depicts or pictures for us in a vivid way some of the dimensions of saving faith. But it need not always be identical to saving faith.

Whatever may be the case with individuals who were healed, the miracles have a connection to the climactic work of Christ in his crucifixion, death, and resurrection. And from there we may observe a link forward to the application of redemption to us in our day. Thus we move from one particular miracle recorded in one of the Gospels to the death and resurrection of Christ, and from there to the application of redemption.

Altogether, we have three instances of the pattern of redemption, namely the miracle, the resurrection of Christ, and the application now. There are two steps linking the instances. In step one, we move from the miracle to the resurrection of Christ. In step two, we move from the resurrection of Christ to its application in the present time. (See figure 5.1.) All of these stages, as we have said, serve the glory of God.

If we wish, we may further expand the area of application to indicate the different kinds of application. Redemption is applied to us at conversion, every day, and at the time of our own bodily resurrection. (See figure 5.2.)

Fig. 5.1: Two Steps to Application

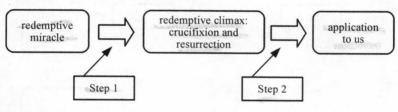

Fig. 5.2: Kinds of Application

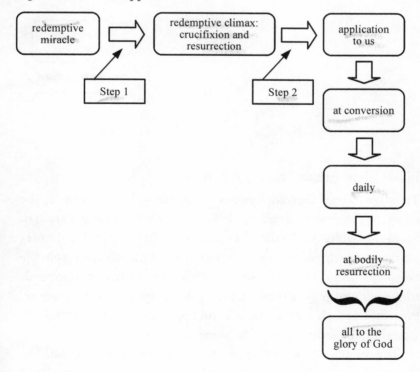

We may also add to the picture the application of redemption to the church as a corporate body. (See fig. 5.3.)

Fig. 5.3: Kinds of Application to the Church

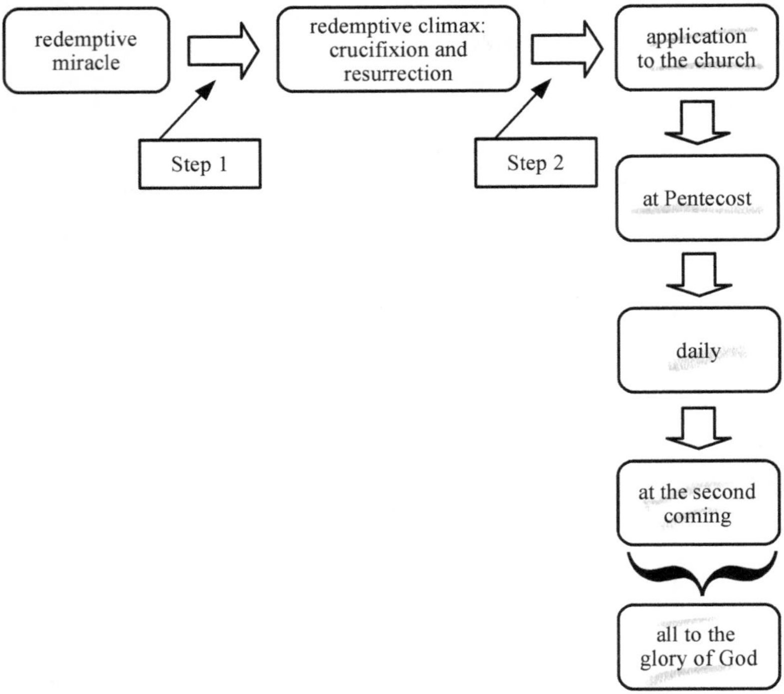

Illustrations of the Threefold Pattern

Thus we have a threefold pattern, consisting in the miracle, the climactic fulfillment of redemption in Christ, and the application to believers—individually (fig. 5.2) and corporately (fig. 5.3) . We may illustrate this threefold pattern using some of the miracles from the Gospel of John. In each case the application of redemption leads to meaningful practical uses of the Bible passage in people's lives. Preachers preach on the passage and apply it to their hearers. Individual Bible readers can do the same.

The miracle of the raising of Lazarus is an easy illustration. The raising of Lazarus is the miracle. The raising of Christ from the dead is the climactic fulfillment. And the granting of new resurrection life to those united to Christ is the application of redemption.

When a preacher preaches on the passage, he should explain how its message points forward to the resurrection of Christ. Christ is now alive, raised from the dead and triumphant forever over the power of death. Christ now has power to give us new life, even as he gave new life to Lazarus when he called him out of the tomb. When Lazarus was dead, Jesus said, "Lazarus, come out!" (John 11:43). Now, through the gospel, Christ says "Come out!" to people today who are dead in sin (Eph. 2:1). And they do come out! They come out, not because they have power in themselves to renew themselves, but because Christ summons them with his divine power, which is also the power of his resurrection.

The passage about the raising of Lazarus calls on us to praise God and to praise Christ who worked the miracle. Praise the Lord for raising Lazarus! Praise him for his compassion and kindness to Martha and Mary, to whom Lazarus was restored! Praise God that Christ was raised from the dead! Praise him for the resurrection life that he gives to us!

It is striking that the passage in John 11 includes a place where Christ praised the Father for the communion he enjoyed with him and for the work that he was about to do:

> And Jesus lifted up his eyes and said, "Father, I thank you that you have heard me. I knew that you always hear me, . . ." (John 11:41–42).

This miracle, like other miracles, displays the glory of God.

Next consider the feeding of the 5,000 and the discourse on the bread of life. The feeding of the 5,000 is the miracle. The provision of redemptive food through Jesus's bodily death is the climactic fulfillment. And believers' feeding on Christ is the application. Praising God and giving glory to God complete the application.

So a preacher will explain not only the miracle but how it points to Christ's redemption and an application to us. Christ's death is a sacrifice for our sins. His resurrection offers forgiveness for sins. To participate, you must feed on Christ. And you do so by faith. So the preacher summons people to faith in Christ. And he summons people who are already Christians to continue feeding on Christ and to deepen their relationship with him.

Every reader and hearer is also summoned by the passage itself. We are being challenged to put our faith in Christ and to depend on Christ alone for the food of eternal life. We respond not only by placing our faith in Christ and feeding on him, but by praising him and rejoicing in the satisfaction and blessing of eternal life. These gifts from Christ display the glory of God.

Consider the healing of the blind man, in John 9. The healing of the man is the miracle. The provision of redemptive light through the revelation of the glory of God in the crucifixion and the resurrection is the climactic fulfillment. The giving of light to believers is the application (cf. 2 Cor. 4:6). This giving of light results in praise and glory to God.

A preacher may explain several aspects of this application. (1) Christ is the light of the world. Through him, and through him alone, you come to know God as you ought to (John 17:3). (2) Christ's light is supremely manifested in his supreme work of redemption, in the crucifixion and resurrection. (3) His light now summons you to respond and come to the light. But you must be healed in order to see. This healing is his provision, and his alone.

Even apart from a preacher, when an individual reader reads the passage, it has the same implications. We receive the light of Christ. We rejoice when we see the glory of Christ. And when we do so, we give glory to God.

Consider the miraculous healing of the sick man, in John 5:1–9. That miracle points to the supreme work of spiritual healing in Jesus's crucifixion and resurrection. The preacher should explain this connection. He also summons his hearers to receive spiritual healing themselves, from Jesus who is still alive and reigning in heaven. Every reader of the Bible should receive this message and take it to heart for himself. Jesus speaks to us, here and now, as we read, and promises spiritual healing to all who come to him in faith. This healing is part of the inaugurated kingdom of God. Not only does he promise it; he brings it about in the lives of those who belong to him. When they receive it, they rejoice and praise him. They give God the glory for this aspect of redemption.

The Importance of Application

The links that go from the miracles to the applications to believers depend on the unity of God's plan and the unity of the way of salvation in Christ. A natural, organic relationship connects the miracles to the death and resurrection of Christ, and connects the work of Christ in turn to those who are being saved throughout the period after the first coming of Christ. We ourselves are in this period. It is the period of international salvation introduced in the book of Acts.

In addition, the connection between miracles and application runs backward into the Old Testament. The salvation depicted in the miracles and accomplished in the crucifixion and resurrection of Christ was applied by God to the saints of the Old Testament. But since we live in the age in which we do, it is proper to be especially concerned with how the Bible applies to us. In dealing with the miracles as signs of redemption, we are not inventing some fanciful or clever application that is not really there. We are following the patterns that God himself has put in place.

Sometimes scholars complain about the use of stories in the Gospels to address modern hearers in an immediate way. They worry that the modern application is overlooking history. Scholars want to make sure that we understand that the miracles happened back then and there in history. The miracles are not merely pictorial lessons that we could use without worrying about whether they ever happened, or whether they are part of God's word. These concerns are legitimate. Christ lived once on earth, in the first century AD and not now. He lived in Palestine, not in modern New York City or Manila or Nairobi.

But there is a complementary truth: Christ is alive now and forever (Heb. 13:8). And the Gospels tell about events back then *for our benefit* and for the glory of God. In many cases, miracles not only depict Christ's climactic work of redemption, but depict it in a way that foreshadows the role played by the human *recipients* of redemption.

When Lazarus was raised from the dead, what happened to him was genuinely analogous to what Christ does for us in his resurrection. It is *also* analogous to what he does *to us* when he gives us new spiritual life, and later when we receive resurrection bodies. Likewise, our experience in receiving the application of redemption has analogies with the experience of the sick man at the Sheep Gate (John 5), with the 5,000 men who ate from the loaves (John 6), and with the people who drank Jesus's wine (John 2).

We are not confusing one event with another. The feeding of the 5,000 is not the same as Jesus giving himself as the bread of life when he dies on the cross, nor is either one of these events the same as our receiving eternal nourishment from him in the present moment. But all three are organically related. And Spirit-guided preachers and Bible readers through the centuries have understood this. It is natural that we should identify with Lazarus—or with Martha and Mary, who receive benefits as well when Lazarus is raised. And when we identify with Lazarus in this way, it issues in praise to God.

6

Typological Reasoning
about Miracles

How do we understand the analogies between the miracles in the Gospels and the great miracle of the resurrection of Christ? In the case of some miracles, like the raising of Lazarus, the connection with the resurrection of Christ is straightforward. In another case, the feeding of the 5,000, the explicit linkages in the Gospel of John between the miracle and Jesus's discourse on the bread of life are a big help. But what if we had only the accounts of the feeding of the 5,000 from the Synoptic Gospels (Matt. 14:13–21; Mark 6:30–44; Luke 9:10–17)? The Synoptic Gospels do not offer as much explicit commentary on the meaning of the miracle. So how do we proceed?

Clowney's Triangle

We may find some help by reflecting on the issue of how to interpret *types*. Roughly speaking, a *type* (as a technical term in theology) is an earthly symbol of a heavenly truth, pointing forward to a fulfillment.[1] Dr. Edmund P. Clowney developed a diagram in the form of the triangle to summarize how to go about interpreting *types* in the Old Testament.[2]

---

[1] Vern S. Poythress, *Reading the Word of God in the Presence of God: A Handbook for Biblical Interpretation* (Wheaton, IL: Crossway, forthcoming), chapter 23. This definition is adapted from a definition I learned from O. Palmer Robertson.

[2] Edmund P. Clowney, *Preaching and Biblical Theology* (Grand Rapids, MI: Eerdmans, 1961), 110.

Jesus's miracles in the Gospels have some affinities to these types in the Old Testament. So we can apply the same insights to them. Clowney's triangle for typology is given in figure 6.1.

Fig. 6.1: Clowney's Triangle

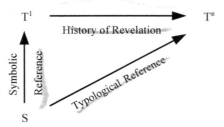

In this triangle, S is the symbol (such as animal sacrifice). T^1 is the truth symbolized by the symbol within its own historical and cultural context. Animal sacrifice symbolizes forgiveness and reconciliation obtained through the death of an innocent substitute. From T^1 an arrow points forward to another item, T^n. T^n means "truth to the nth power," the climactic fulfillment of truth in Christ. In the case of animal sacrifice, the truth concerns the fact that Christ died as our substitute, in order to bring forgiveness of sins and reconciliation with God. The symbol S is a *type*, pointing forward to the fulfillment in Christ as represented by T^n. The diagonal line from S to T^n is accordingly labeled "Typological Reference."[3] When applied to animal sacrifices as a type, Clowney's triangle is represented in fig. 6.2.

The main point in using Clowney's triangle is to proceed in our reflections using two steps rather than one. In step 1 we think about the vertical leg of the triangle, moving from the symbol S to the truth it represents, T^1. In step 2 we move forward in history to the fulfillment in a climactic manifestation of the truth, T^n. By this means we attempt to do justice to the way in which the symbol functions in its original historical context (S in relation to T^1). By contrast, someone

---

[3] Clowney's original publication used the label "Typical Reference." The designation "Typical Reference" is technically correct. In this context, the word *typical* means "having to do with a type." But the word is likely to be misunderstood as having another meaning, "exhibiting the common characteristics of a group." For clarity, I have substituted the word *typological*.

who "leaps" directly from a symbol to fulfillment in Christ may end up doing it in an artificial or arbitrary way, because he is not paying attention to the meaning that the symbol had even at an earlier period. The alleged "meaning" that he finds then gets detached from the meaning that was understood when the symbol was first given.

Fig. 6.2: Clowney's Triangle for Animal Sacrifice

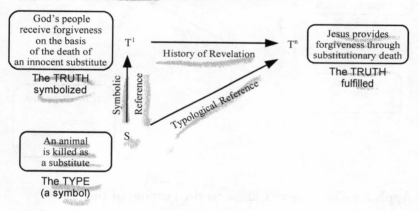

For example, when a person reads about wood in the Old Testament, he might make a "leap" directly to the cross of Christ. It is true enough that the cross was made of wood. But we need to ask how the mention of wood in the Old Testament served the people to whom God was speaking at the time. Deuteronomy 29:17 mentions "idols of *wood* and stone." In this verse, the point of wood—and stone—is that it is foolish to make idols and worship something that has been made, something created. We miss the real meaning if we just make a "leap." Christ died on a cross of wood, but it is inappropriate to see a direct reference to the cross in this occurrence of wood. The two-step process encourages us, in the first step, not to get side-tracked but to ask what God was saying in the original context.

As we saw in the preceding chapter, the accomplishment of redemption in Christ has an organic relationship to the *application* of redemption to believers. If we wish, we can add another part to Clowney's triangle, to remind ourselves of the importance of application.[4] The application can be represented by a line moving downward from fulfillment in Christ, as in fig. 6.3:

Fig. 6.3: Clowney's Triangle for Animal Sacrifice, with Application

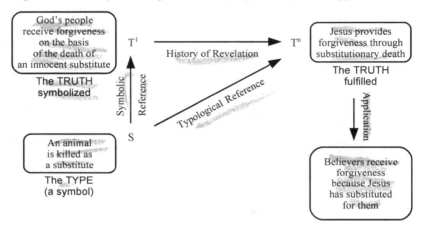

Applying Clowney's Triangle to the Feeding of the 5,000

The same principles apply to the miracles of Jesus in the Gospels. As we have seen, the miracles are "signs." They signify meanings about Jesus and his redemption. The people who observed the miracles during Jesus's earthly life could figure out some of the meaning, at least if they had spiritual discernment. The meaning then unfolded further as history moved forward to the crucifixion and resurrection of Christ.

In this situation, the miracle itself, such as the feeding of the 5,000, is the symbol S. The meaning of the miracle that is discernible at the time is its truth content, T^1. In the case of the feeding of the 5,000, this meaning is that God through Jesus supplies *spiritual* nourishment, not merely food for the stomach (the symbol). The climactic truth T^n is the meaning seen in the light of Jesus's crucifixion and resurrection. Jesus himself is the food, and the food he offers comes on the basis of his sacrificial death and his resurrection, so that by communion with him we enjoy the eternal life that he has

---

[4] I believe that someone later than Edmund Clowney got the idea of adding to the triangle another line, pointing to application. I am not sure who did this first.

in his resurrected state. We can then fill in the triangle diagram as it applies to the feeding of the 5,000, as in figure 6.4.

Fig. 6.4: Clowney's Triangle for Feeding the 5,000

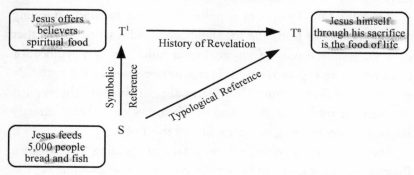

How do we know that the feeding with physical bread symbolizes feeding with spiritual food (the vertical leg of the triangle)? In John 6, we know it because Jesus explicitly explained the significance in his discourse on the bread of life. But could people have seen the same thing with only the information given them in one of the accounts in the Synoptic Gospels?

The background in the Old Testament helps. Multiple texts form the background for the feeding of the 5,000. God gave the manna to Israel in the wilderness (cf. Ex. 16:9–36). He explicitly connected the manna with the principle of living by the word of God: "man does not live by bread alone, but man lives by every word that comes from the mouth of the LORD" (Deut. 8:3). God enabled Elisha the prophet to preside over a special multiplication of bread, in which a hundred men were fed from "twenty loaves of barley and fresh ears of grain" (2 Kings 4:42). Through Elijah God gave a miraculous provision for the widow of Zarephath (1 Kings 17:8–16). Through Elisha he brought relief from famine (2 Kings 7:1–20).

All these accounts fit together with a larger picture in which God promises to be the all-sufficient supplier of needs to those who trust him. The context of God's character shows that the provision of physical needs expresses a deeper commitment on God's part to supply *all* needs. And the deepest needs are spiritual. In spite of the provision of manna, most of the people of Israel died in the wilderness because of their unbelief. They needed a change of heart, not merely food for their stomachs.

Thus the Old Testament supplies a context for understanding the significance of Jesus and the significance of his work. Given that context, Jesus's supply of physical food functions as a symbol for comprehensive supply of need. Hunger for physical food naturally points to the deeper hunger for spiritual nourishment. The explicit discourse in John 6 on the bread of life draws out what is already implicit in the meaning of the feeding of the 5,000.

Using Clowney's triangle is important for guiding us to discern the meaning built into a miracle instead of imposing meaning on it in an arbitrary way. The first leg of the triangle, the vertical leg, which represents step 1 in the process of analysis, asks about the meaning of a miracle in its immediate context and in the context of the Old Testament. Each miracle is a miracle *in a context*. It is not merely a free-standing story, which might be used to illustrate a redemptive principle regardless of the origin of the story or regardless of its historicity.

As a final step, we can add to Clowney's triangle the role of application. We receive Jesus as the bread of life when we trust in him and are united to him for salvation. As we continue to believe in him, we continue to feed on him. See fig. 6.5.

Fig. 6.5: Clowney's Triangle for Feeding the 5,000, with Application

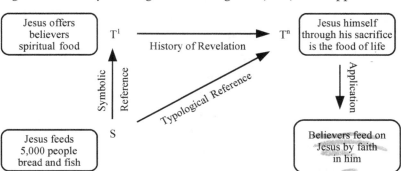

The Healing of the Man Blind from Birth

We can use Clowney's triangle again in looking at the miracle of the healing of the man blind from birth, as recorded in John 9.

First, in step 1, represented by the vertical leg of Clowney's triangle, we ask about the meaning of the miracle in its immediate context. Jesus said, "I am the light of the world" (John 9:5; cf. 8:12). And by the end of John 9 he addressed directly the issue of spiritual blindness on the part of Jewish leaders (9:39–41). So it is clear that physical healing, which restores physical sight, symbolizes spiritual healing restoring spiritual sight.

Second, we consider step 2, represented by the horizontal leg of Clowney's triangle. This step considers how the meaning points to a climactic fulfillment in Christ's death and resurrection. This step is not too hard, because the crucifixion and the resurrection form two phases of the climactic revelation of the significance of Christ and his life, and the redemptive significance of his person and work. The resurrection shows the glory of the Father and of the Son.

Putting these two steps together, we arrive at a summary as represented in fig. 6.6.

Fig. 6.6: Clowney's Triangle for the Man Blind from Birth

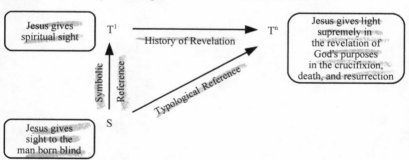

We can also add application to the triangle (see fig. 6.7). How does the light of Christ apply to believers? Believers receive light as they look in faith on Christ, who was raised up on the cross and then raised up in his resurrection (John 3:14–15).

Fig. 6.7: Clowney's Triangle for the Man Blind from Birth, with Application

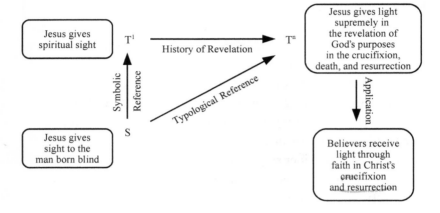

7

Broader Implications of
the Miracles of Jesus

The meanings found in Jesus's miracles have broader implications. The miracles already have meaning at the narrow time and place at which they happened. They also have implications for the larger vistas of the history of redemption.

Broader Implications of Feeding the 5,000

We may illustrate using the miracle of the feeding of the 5,000. As we indicated in the previous chapters, this miracle expresses the principle of God supplying spiritual food. We can picture the broader implications of this principle as smaller and bigger circles of meaning.

The smallest circle is the circle of the immediate circumstances in the feeding of the 5,000.[1] In these circumstances, Jesus provided both physical food and spiritual food. The spiritual food took the form of the symbolic meaning provided in the physical act of feeding. In addition, in the Gospel of John the symbolic meaning was explicitly interpreted on the next day, when Jesus gave the discourse on the bread of life.

---

[1] In fig. 7.1 and subsequent "Circles of Meaning" illustrations, the innermost "circle" is actually depicted as a "rounded rectangle," to better accommodate the enclosed text.

The next wider circle is the circle of Jesus's earthly ministry as a whole. Jesus offered spiritual food through his teaching, of which the discourse on the bread of life was one key instance. He also provided spiritual food through his other miracles, because these too have symbolic significance; they are signs of redemption. He provided spiritual food in his own person, since his very presence on earth was a coming of the spiritual bread—which he himself is—from heaven to earth, like the Old Testament supply of manna.

The next wider circle encompasses Jesus's death and resurrection as well as his earlier earthly ministry. Jesus's crucifixion, death, and resurrection were the climactic works that he did on earth. So they can be included within his earthly ministry. But they are so important and serve so much as the hinge of history that it is worthwhile to distinguish them from the rest of his earthly ministry, and to reflect more intently on how their significance has connections with the earlier miracles. In the case of the feeding of the 5,000, the decisive feeding with spiritual food took place in Jesus's death and resurrection, since his death was a sacrificial death and his body then became the source of spiritual nourishment. We receive the benefits of his death and resurrection. This process is the fulfillment of the Old Testament ceremonies where the Israelites ate part of the flesh of the peace offerings, signifying their participation in the benefits from the sacrifice of the peace offerings (Lev. 7:15–16).

The next wider circle consists in the age of gospel proclamation, from the day of Pentecost onward to the close of this age, the second coming of Christ. During this age the gospel is going out to the ends of the earth (Acts 1:8). It calls forth a response in the form of spiritual transformation and faith in Christ. Through faith, believers feed on Christ. In this sense, Christ who reigns in heaven is continually supplying spiritual food. He gives it not to 5,000 people, but to all who believe in him—far more than 5,000. And this feeding takes place through a kind of "multiplication." It is not the multiplication of physical loaves, but of the gospel itself, as it spreads:

And the word of God *continued to increase*, and the number of the disciples *multiplied* greatly in Jerusalem, and a great many of the priests became obedient to the faith. (Acts 6:7)

But the word of God *increased* and *multiplied*. (Acts 12:24)

And the word of the Lord *was spreading* throughout the whole region. (Acts 13:49)

. . . so that from Jerusalem and all the way around to Illyricum I have *fulfilled* the ministry of the gospel of Christ. (Rom. 15:19)

The number of the disciples multiplies. But, in addition, the gospel bears fruit in the individual lives of disciples. There is growth in knowing and obeying Christ. Disciples bring forth the fruit of the Holy Spirit: "love, joy, peace, patience, kindness, goodness, faithfulness, gentleness, self-control" (Gal. 5:22–23).

Food in Creation and Re-Creation

The broadest circle of implications includes the entirety of redemptive history, issuing in the consummation. At the consummation, the multiplication of the gospel has reached its consummation, with the gathering of all nations:

By its light will the *nations* walk, and the kings of the earth will bring their glory into it, . . . (Rev. 21:24; cf. 7:9)

Everlasting nourishment is supplied, as represented by the tree of life:

. . . also, on either side of the river, the tree of life with its twelve kinds of fruit, yielding its fruit each month. (Rev. 22:2)

The connection with the river of life, "flowing from the throne of God and of the Lamb" (22:1), symbolically reminds us that the source of this nourishment is in God himself and the Lamb. The passage about the marriage supper of the Lamb makes the same theological point using different imagery (19:9).

The imagery of the tree of life also takes us back through its associations to the original order of creation. According to Genesis 2, the tree of life stood "in the midst of the garden" of Eden, the garden of God (Gen. 2:9; cf. Ezek. 28:13). The theme of spiritual nourishment spans all of history, from the original garden of Eden to the final garden-city of the new Jerusalem (Rev. 21:9–22:5). Physical nourishment, given by all the fruit trees in the garden of Eden, is a wonderful benefit from God. Since it is connected to God who gives it, the physical nourishment is a token of God's favor, and of the spiritual nourishment that he provides through communion with him. Before the fall, Adam and Eve would have experienced the two together. Eating physical food is itself an experience of God's goodness, and evokes thanksgiving to God, which is a form of spiritual communion. The one not only signifies the other, but embodies it. The tree of life, of course, was a special tree, which expressed the idea of spiritual communion and spiritual life more intensely.

The feeding of the 5,000 thus unites creation and redemption. God created trees. God created barley, and the human ability to make barley into loaves. God as creator is the source of the five barley loaves with which the miracle starts. Every year, through growth and harvest, God multiplies barley and wheat and other grains, and at harvest people enjoy his bounty. The miraculous feeding of the 5,000 compresses these processes into a few moments. It points to the power of Christ the Redeemer, as we have said. But it also builds on the realities of what God does as creator. Christ is mediator of creation as well as mediator of redemption (Col. 1:15–20). So creation and re-creation enjoy an organic relation to each other, through Christ. It is fitting that their relationship should be manifested in miracles, such as the feeding of the 5,000.

Old Testament Background for the Feeding of the 5,000

In addition to these connections, we have still further connections with themes in the Old Testament. We mentioned earlier that the feeding of the 5,000 is analogous to God's supply of manna from heaven during the time when Israel was in the wilderness (John

6:32–33). It is also analogous to an Old Testament miracle in which Elisha saw to it that a hundred men were fed with "twenty loaves of barley and fresh ears of grain" (2 Kings 4:42–44). Through Elijah's word, the widow of Zarephath had a miraculous supply of food "for many days" (1 Kings 17:8–16). Through the word of Elisha, Israel was able to experience relief from famine due to a siege (2 Kings 7:1). Through Joseph, people were delivered from seven years of famine in Egypt (Gen. 41:53–57). In general, famine or abundance of food come as a result of curses or blessings of the Lord (Deut. 28:3–8, 11–12, 16–18, 22–24, 53–57).

For a summary of all the circles of meaning for this miracle, see figure 7.1.

Consider the circle containing the spread of the gospel in the book of Acts. The gospel continues to spread during this age. This circle indicates that the miracles imply applications to us, since we are in the redemptive period represented by this circle—the period extending from Pentecost to the second coming. During this period, the gospel itself proclaims the meaning of the miracles. In a broad sense, the meaning or significance of miracles includes their implications, which in turn includes application to us. Each of us is invited to come to Christ for spiritual food.

All of these circles display the glory of God, and should lead to praising God.

The Significance of the Healing of the Man Born Blind

We can plot a similar series of expanding circles for the healing of the man born blind. The smallest circle consists in Jesus actually healing the blind man. This healing had a physical and a spiritual side. The blind man received physical sight, and he received spiritual sight when he came to believe in Jesus (John 9:38). Next, Jesus's entire earthly ministry was a ministry of bringing the light of redemptive revelation. His purpose of bringing light came to a climax in his crucifixion and resurrection. These climactic events, above all, are what God uses in the proclamation of the gospel to open blind eyes.

Fig. 7.1: Circles of Meaning for the Feeding of the 5,000

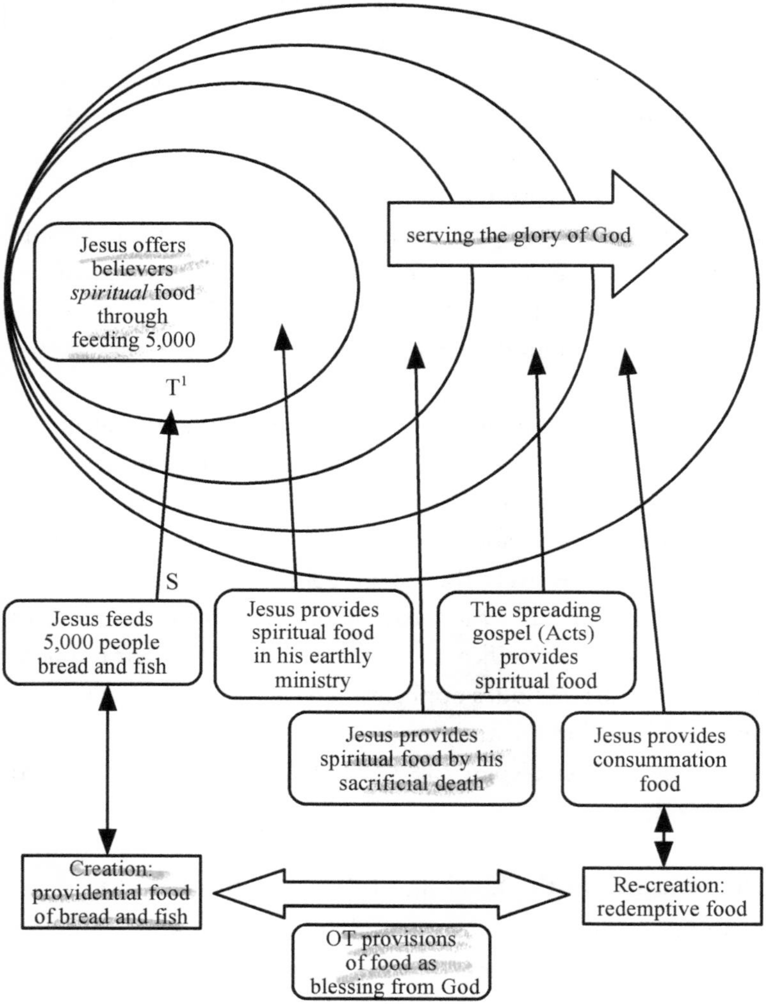

Next, the book of Acts shows how God opens blind eyes during the gospel age:

But rise and stand upon your feet, for I have appeared to you for this purpose, to appoint you as a servant and witness to the things in which you have *seen* me and to those in which I will ap-

pear to you, delivering you from your people and from the Gentiles—to whom I am sending you to *open their eyes*, so that they
may turn *from darkness to light* and from the power of Satan to
God, that they may receive forgiveness of sins and a place among
those who are sanctified by faith in me. (Acts 26:16–18)

. . . he would *proclaim light* both to our people and to the Gentiles. (Acts 26:23)

Finally, the consummation brings healing of all physical dis-
abilities, including blindness, and gives to the saints the supreme
spiritual vision of the face of God:

They will *see his face*, and his name will be on their foreheads.
(Rev. 22:4)

The Old Testament offers several instances that form a background for John 9. For example, Isaiah 35:5 indicates that the climactic time of redemption will include healing of the blind:

Then the eyes of the blind shall be opened,
  and the ears of the deaf unstopped.

Jesus's use of clay in healing has a resonance with Genesis 2:7,
where "the LORD God formed man of dust from the ground." Jesus
was performing an act of giving new life, in a manner analogous to
God's act of creation.[2]

The theme of light in John 9 has links with God creating light
on day one of the creation week (Gen. 1:3; cf. John 1:4–5), with
the redemptive light of the pillar of cloud and fire (Num. 9:15–23),
and with the spiritual light of God that he gives for redemption and
guidance (Ps. 27:1; 36:9; 43:3; 119:105; Isa. 9:2).[3]

There is also a link from John 9 to the healing of Naaman the
Syrian (2 Kings 5:9–14). Both Naaman and the blind man had to go

---

[2] "Jesus is the One who fulfills all the hopes of Israel, the One who brings new life from the dead clay
with breath and water from his mouth" (Peter J. Leithart, *Deep Exegesis: The Mystery of Reading
Scripture* [Waco, TX: Baylor University Press, 2009], 73).
[3] Ibid., 72.

and wash in order to be healed. And in both cases the act of washing seemed pointless—why would Elisha or Jesus give instructions to go and wash if he could have healed the man on the spot?[4] We may not know all the reasons why washing is part of the process. But we may see at least some reasons. In both cases the instructions underscore the sovereignty of God's ways. People must do as he says, even if they do not understand it. And in both cases the act of washing symbolizes cleansing. In this way healing gets linked with the larger purpose of God's salvation and God's kingdom, which includes both healing and cleansing, especially cleansing from sin. In sum, Jesus's healing of the blind man is linked to the Old Testament healing of Naaman through the prophet Elisha. This link confirms that Jesus's work fulfills the acts of healing in the Old Testament, and also that Jesus fulfills the Old Testament office of the prophet.

The series of circles of implications is summarized in figure 7.2.

Once again, the circle including the spread of the gospel in Acts also includes *us*. The miracle of Jesus healing the blind man implies that each of us should receive spiritual sight from Christ, and be able to see "the light of the knowledge of the glory of God in the face of Jesus Christ" (2 Cor. 4:6). All these aspects display the glory of God. Praise to God for the richness of his grace and wisdom, through all of time!

Multiple Thematic Connections

Other miracles of Jesus show a similar multiplicity of connections. They take place against the background of God's work of creation and providence; they resonate with miracles, promises, and other themes in the Old Testament; they look forward to the consummation. We would take up much space if we explored all these kinds of connections with every miracle. For the most part, in the remaining chapters we will concentrate on the connections with the heart of redemption, which is found in the crucifixion, death, resurrection, and ascension of Christ. We will also include brief remarks about

---

[4] Ibid., 73.

the ways in which Christ's miracles fulfill Old Testament promises and Old Testament patterns of redemption.

Fig. 7.2: Circles of Meaning for the Healing of the Man Born Blind

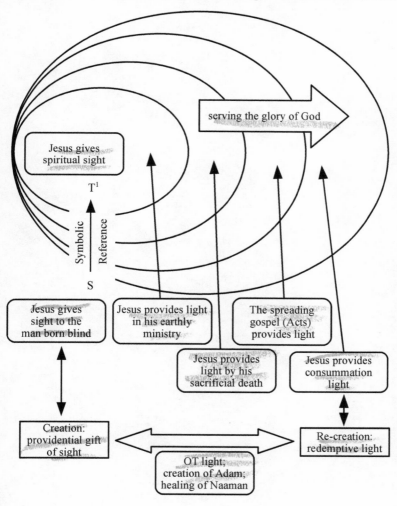

8

Specific Applications

In chapter 5 we observed that the miracles symbolize Christ's redemptive work, and that therefore they have natural, organic applications to believers. We were thinking mostly of applying the meaning of each miracle to a believer's life as a whole. But do the miracles also have significance that may apply to specific circumstances in a person's life? Let us consider this question carefully.

Consider again the resurrection of Lazarus. It symbolizes the truth that Christ gives new spiritual life to those who believe in him. And at the second coming believers will receive resurrection bodies. Such benefits do not come to every human being, but only to those who believe in Christ, those who put their trust in him. But we can still see a kind of application that extends to all who hear the gospel. The gospel summons unbelievers to place their trust in Christ and receive new life from him. The picture of Jesus raising Lazarus offers a vivid illustration or analogy, which unbelievers are invited to consider, and then to apply to themselves, on the condition that they come to faith in Jesus. The story of Lazarus commands those who begin in unbelief to cast off unbelief and come to Christ to receive eternal life.

In addition, as we saw earlier, the pattern of death and new life has repeated application to Christian believers. The pattern belongs to conversion, when we die with Christ as symbolized in baptism (Rom. 6:3–4). It belongs to the final resurrection of the body (1 Cor. 15:45–49). And Scripture indicates that the pattern applies every day:

> . . . always carrying in the body *the death of Jesus*, so that *the life of Jesus* may also be manifested in our bodies. For we who live are *always* being given over to *death* for Jesus' sake, so that *the life of Jesus* also may be manifested in our mortal flesh. So *death* is at work in us, but *life* in you. (2 Cor. 4:10–12)

> I protest, brothers, by my pride in you, which I have in Christ Jesus our Lord, I *die* every day! (1 Cor. 15:31)

These verses indicate that the basic pattern of redemption, the redemptive plot, has daily applications.

Washing Dishes

Let us consider, then, how to apply the story of the resurrection of Lazarus to some more ordinary situations. First, suppose that Joe is washing dishes, for the umpteenth time, and is feeling bored with it. He is getting restless and complaining: "Why should I be tied down here rather than doing something interesting like watching football on TV or being creative in woodworking?" Or maybe he has some "spiritual" alternative: "God, why do you have me here instead of doing some great things in Bible study or evangelism?" Either way, he is falling into discontent and complaining.

So can the story of Lazarus apply to him and his situation? Joe feels trapped in meaningless activity, which is no better than total inactivity. It feels worthless. It may not seem to be a big thing, but it is a small case of life shriveling up, and therefore represents in a small-scale way the process of dying emotionally. In comparison with "real living," Joe is like Lazarus in the tomb. So he has a kind of longing for a redemptive story or a redemptive plot to operate in his life.

As in many cases of discontent, Joe sees his difficulty as coming from his circumstances. "I'm tied to the kitchen sink, with a mound of dishes." But a deeper difficulty lies in Joe himself. His feelings are in many ways understandable. But are they combined with self-centeredness, according to which he is defining "real life" as self-fulfillment in activities that he could choose? Even if he would choose Bible study or evangelism, would it be with a sense of pride in the satisfaction of being "great" as a Christian because he is doing "the Lord's work"? So the story of Lazarus applies to Joe by applying the work of the death and resurrection of Christ. Joe must die daily to selfish ambition. In addition, he must receive new life through Christ to live for God. If a first-century slave can serve Christ, so can he:

> Bondservants [slaves], obey in everything those who are your earthly masters, not by way of eye-service, as people-pleasers, but with sincerity of heart, fearing the Lord. Whatever you do, work heartily, as for the Lord and not for men, knowing that from the Lord you will receive the inheritance as your reward. You are serving the Lord Christ. (Col. 3:22–24)

So Joe prays, "Lord, let me live for *you*, whether other people notice it or not" ("not . . . people-pleasers"). The Holy Spirit supplies Joe with spiritual power to serve faithfully in what is seemingly insignificant.

And what is Joe doing? Cleaning dirty dishes. It can seem boring, partly because it has to be done again and again, after every meal. But in the plan of God, cleaning has a definite purpose. Without cleaning, people might eat contaminated food and get sick and die. Through the power of God, and the wisdom of God that he has imparted concerning cleanness, Joe is playing his part in the continued pattern to rescue people from sickness and death. He is helping to "clean" the world. And the world will become definitively clean in the new heaven and new earth, which Christ will bring. The most focused work of cleaning comes in the triumph of life over death, because death is the final "uncleanness." Joe's work is a small application of the power of Christ's resurrection. It does have weighty significance.

Is this application fanciful? It might seem so, if we have not filled in enough steps in inference. But we should remember that Christ's resurrection is the foundation not only for the renewal of the physical body of human beings but for the renewal of the cosmos itself, when "the creation itself will be set free from its bondage to corruption and obtain the freedom of the glory of the children of God" (Rom. 8:21). The resurrection is really the foundation for all benefits from God, including small benefits. And the benefit of clean dishes and clean food is one small benefit. As Joe participates in this small benefit, he can praise God through Christ for the privilege of washing dishes.

Disciplining a Child

As a second case, consider Sue. She has discovered her four-year-old son, Tim, with his hand in the cookie jar, ready to steal a cookie. How does the raising of Lazarus apply to her? How does it apply to Tim?

Let us suppose that Sue is a Christian parent who understands her responsibility to discipline Tim as part of her larger responsibility to teach him the Christian way. But she finds conflicting motives in her heart. Along with her righteous anger over sin she finds also unrighteous anger: she is angry because Tim has made it difficult for her. He has interfered with her plans, and she resents it. She has to interrupt what she has planned to do in order to deal with him. And if she is going to discipline him responsibly, it will take time. She will have to talk with him and pray with him, not just give him a swat on the hand and say "no." Along with anger she also has laziness. Part of her says, "Just let it go this time. You have more important things to do."

So Sue has to deal with sin that shows itself in her attitudes. God calls on her to die to sin and live to righteousness. Christ in raising Lazarus speaks to her also. Christ said, "Lazarus, come out" (John 11:43). In application, he says to Sue, "Come out"—come out from the spiritual deadness of corrupt motives, and into the spiritual life of new motives that are fitting for serving God. He calls Sue to bless God for the honor of imitating God's fatherly care by exercising motherly discipline:

And have you forgotten the exhortation that addresses you as sons?

"My son, do not regard lightly the discipline of the Lord,
    nor be weary when reproved by him.
For the Lord disciplines the one he loves,
and chastises every son whom he receives."

It is for discipline that you have to endure. God is treating you as sons. For what son is there whom his father does not discipline? (Heb. 12:5–7)

If Sue responds to the grace of God, she is living out a redemptive plot. The plot starts in the normal situation of a peaceful home. Then a difficulty raises its head: Tim's hand has gotten into the cookie jar. And a complication ensues: Sue's own motives are corrupted. Sue meets the climax as she confronts her own sinful motives. She cries out to God, and God delivers her into new blessing and new commitment to carry out the discipline in the strength of the Lord. The redemptive plot has reached resolution.

In addition, Sue has to try to communicate to her son the meaning of new living in Christ. The message to the son is not simply, "Ask forgiveness," and "Don't do it again"—though these are part of the process. The message is also that Christ raised Lazarus as a picture of what he does for you. You are to die to the selfish desire for another cookie, which you snatch in disobedience, and rise to the new life of resisting temptation in the power of the Holy Spirit and finding fulfillment in doing the will of God. Sue has to try to explain this message in language that a four-year-old can understand. But pictures, like the picture of Lazarus being raised, actually help, by making vivid and concrete the promise of new life.

As Tim receives instruction from his mother, a redemptive plot works out in his life as well. The plot travels from normality to a sinful trap, and then onward to deliverance. Both Sue and Tim may learn to praise God in the midst of their difficulties and tears, because God is at work in them, and is bringing the resurrection life of Christ into their lives to transform them.

Failing a Test

Consider another example. Dave has just failed a chemistry test. Dave is a non-Christian. He comes to commiserate with Ken, who is a Christian classmate. As Dave reveals his discouragement, he also begins to indicate that there is more depth in it. Dave has his heart set on being a doctor after he finishes his premed work. Does his failure on the test mean that he won't make it through chemistry, and that his plans for being a doctor will fall apart? What does Ken say in response to Dave's misery? Can Ken tell the story of Lazarus in a way that applies to Dave?

Ken's first job is surely to listen and to sympathize with Dave's feelings of discouragement and depression. Life is not always easy. It includes failures as well as successes. Dave's failure is bad enough. But the ultimate failure—for everyone—is death, which is what we see in the story of Lazarus. The story of Lazarus applies because every failure is a small-scale analogue to the ultimate failure of death. Jesus raised Lazarus, and that is a symbol of his power to overcome every failure that ever confronts us in our lives.

Ken cannot promise Dave that being a Christian is a kind of magic wand that will sweetly dissolve all problems and give Dave whatever he wants. Maybe Dave just does not have the intellectual ability to master chemistry and other premed requirements. New life in Christ does not mean magically giving Dave an escape from his intellectual limitations. On the other hand, maybe Dave has failed because he is lazy or undisciplined, but he does not want to look frankly at these underlying causes. In either case, new life in Christ provides an ultimate foundation for living through the smaller failures of life. New life in Christ may lead eventually to Dave finding another vocational goal. Or it may lead to Dave overcoming his lack of discipline.

Fellowship with Christ will help him. But Dave has to look at other issues. Underneath Dave's desire to be a doctor there are almost certainly mixed motives. Dave wants to serve other people and to make a difference in their lives. But he also wants personal satisfaction and the admiration of others for his success. He wants to become rich through his work. These desires have a selfish aspect. Like everyone else, Dave is a sinner before God, and he needs forgiveness and reconciliation with God.

The raising of Lazarus is relevant to Dave, because Dave is dead in sin. That spiritual deadness is at the root of everything else. But in addition, Dave is experiencing a kind of metaphorical death over the failed exam. He finds himself at the bottom, in an emotional pit. Christ commands him to come out, to experience new life. The new life is fundamentally new spiritual life in communion with Christ. But this new life also alters the way Dave approaches a failed test and the discipline of studying for the chemistry course. If God works regeneration in Dave's heart, Dave's desire becomes first of all the desire to serve Christ. And then that desire flows over into being willing to suffer, and seeing that failure in chemistry is endurable when Christ is with him. It also means putting effort into chemistry, and maybe being willing to take the course a second time and receive tutoring, depending on the situation. It also means leaving in the hands of Christ the ultimate issue of whether Dave will become a doctor. Dave no longer makes that goal into an idol that he could not bear to give up.

There is a small-scale redemptive plot in Dave's life. Normality has descended into failure in the chemistry test. What will lift Dave out? Fundamentally, new life. But there are also plots relating to David's lack of discipline, or his selfish desires, or his making an idol of the goal of being a doctor. The raising of Lazarus has analogies with the whole pattern of being raised "from dead works to serve the living God" (Heb. 9:14). David is being invited, not only to come to Christ for new life, but also to begin to live a life of praising God, not serving his own selfish desires.

An Exciting Date

The relevance of Lazarus extends not only to crises but also to happiness. Let us suppose that Jane is anticipating her first date with a boy, Carl, in whom she has been interested for some time. Jane is happy and pictures for herself the delight of a very fulfilling relationship. Jane is a non-Christian, who talks about her coming date with her Christian friend Carol. What might Carol say?

Carol may sympathize. But she can also try to see how the raising of Lazarus speaks to this happy situation. Jane is happy because she pictures for herself a new life in the form of an exciting romantic relationship with Carl. She is producing in her mind a redemptive plot. How so? She may or may not have been depressed previously because she did not have a boyfriend, or because she could not manage to get Carl's attention. Whatever her previous situation, she pictures the coming developments as a great upward trend. She is being "redeemed" or "delivered," figuratively speaking, from loneliness. She hopes that she will be lavished with love, satisfaction, excitement, and bliss. This redemptive plot is analogous to the raising of Lazarus. Jane hopes to find new life with Carl, in a way that probably will make her previous life seem like death in comparison.

What makes Jane's anticipation of romance so exciting? Romance is a powerful experience in human life. It is so powerful precisely because it analogically mirrors the fascination, intimacy, and blessing that arises in God's relationship to his people, which in both the Old Testament and the New is depicted as marriage (Hosea 3:1; Isa. 54:5; 62:4–5; etc.). But if human romance becomes a substitute for relationship with God, it will fail. No human partner can fill the void that only God can fill.

So what will be Carol's response to Jane? Carol can be positively excited about the blessing that God is giving to Jane in this relationship. At the same time, Carol can gently say to Jane that, if she does not receive the new adventure *as* a blessing from God that points to even deeper sources of blessing, she will find herself eventually disappointed and frustrated even with the most promising partner.

So Jane needs to move from spiritual death to spiritual life, through the resurrection of Christ, in order that her romantic relationships themselves may be renewed. Jane needs to turn from "dead," selfish relationships in which she is subtly or not so subtly exploiting her partner, and be raised to a new life that transforms the way in which she looks at men and pursues romance. An approach that starts with the premise "It's all about me" lies in the realm of spiritual death.

Using Other Miracles

The raising of Lazarus is only one of many miracles. All of the miracles point to the great miracle of the resurrection of Christ. At the same time, each miracle is unique. And some miracles by their uniqueness may more effectively suggest applications to some specific life situations. For example, Jesus turned the water into wine at a wedding feast. So the theme of wedding and marriage links it more closely to Jane's hoped-for romantic relationship. The feeding of the 5,000 raises the issue of how best to live life abundantly. Jesus is "the bread of *life*." So that story might serve as a starting point when talking about Dave's hopes to live a fulfilling life by becoming a doctor. Jesus's healing of the leper in Matthew 8:1–4 raises the theme of what is clean versus what is unclean. So it might be the starting point for Joe's reflections on washing dishes. In Matthew 8:1–4 Jesus cleansed the leper from uncleanness. By analogy, Joe has been given the privilege of cleansing the dishes from uncleanness. And this cleansing contributes to the health of his family. If Joe is serving the Lord and imitating him in this small way, his work has significance.

We can find much potential for many applications, because any one miracle embodies general principles of redemption. It points to the central truths of Jesus's accomplishment. And we all need redemption. We need it not only in the big sense, as whole people; we need it in the small crevices of particular circumstances such as washing dishes and disciplining children.

Part III

MIRACLES IN MATTHEW

9

The Virgin Birth
(Matthew 1:18–25)

Now let us begin to go through the Gospel of Matthew and seek to understand the significance of the miracles recorded there. We will use the principles we have already developed primarily with reference to the Gospel of John.

The Gospel of John has more explicit instruction about the significance of some of the main miracles, like the feeding of the 5,000. But miracles in the other Gospels have significance in similar ways. It just takes a more careful look at the miracles to see their significance. The miracles in Matthew, like those in John, are signs of the kingdom of God. In the life of Jesus we see the beginning of God's saving reign in salvation, as prophesied and foreshadowed in the Old Testament. The unity of God's saving purposes in the rule of his kingdom leads to the conclusion that the miracles in Matthew are organically connected to the climax of the kingdom in Jesus's death and resurrection.

In addition, the Gospel of Matthew, like the Gospel of John, is a narrative, and its very structure leads forward to the crucifixion and the resurrection. This narrative structure helps to underscore the theological unity in God's kingdom work.

In our discussion so far, we have focused on miracles that Jesus performed. But an expanded viewpoint can encompass miracles that take place with Jesus as the recipient. The virgin conception and birth in Matthew 1:18–25 and the miracles at Jesus's baptism in Matthew 3:13–17 are among these miracles. In this chapter we consider the virgin birth:

> Now the birth of Jesus Christ took place in this way. When his mother Mary had been betrothed to Joseph, before they came together she was found to be with child from the Holy Spirit. And her husband Joseph, being a just man and unwilling to put her to shame, resolved to divorce her quietly. But as he considered these things, behold, an angel of the Lord appeared to him in a dream, saying, "Joseph, son of David, do not fear to take Mary as your wife, for that which is conceived in her is from the Holy Spirit. She will bear a son, and you shall call his name Jesus, for he will save his people from their sins." All this took place to fulfill what the Lord had spoken by the prophet:
>
> > "Behold, the virgin shall conceive and bear a son,
> > and they shall call his name Immanuel"
>
> (which means, God with us). When Joseph woke from sleep, he did as the angel of the Lord commanded him: he took his wife, but knew her not until she had given birth to a son. And he called his name Jesus. (Matt. 1:18–25)

The Significance of the Virgin Birth

The virgin conception and birth of Jesus inaugurated the climactic period in history, the period in which God accomplished salvation through the work of Jesus. Matthew indicates specifically that the virgin conception fulfills the prophecy in Isaiah 7:14 (cf. Matt. 1:22–23). The name given to Jesus announces salvation:

> She will bear a son, and you shall call his name Jesus, *for he will save his people from their sins.* (Matt. 1:21)

The virgin conception therefore represents the opening miracle of a whole redemptive epoch. Its miraculous character underscored the fact that God was working, and that it takes spectacular and startling works of God to bring about the decisive remedy for the deepest roots and destructive aspects of sin. The initial miracle of virgin conception prepares readers for a continuing narrative that will include a whole series of miracles.

Why a virgin conception? A miracle is a suitable inauguration for the epoch of kingdom fulfillment, but why *this* miracle? The absence of normal means for conception underscored the presence of God, who must radically take the initiative. The virgin birth also broke the pattern of human beings inheriting guilt and sinfulness from Adam.[1] The incarnation of Christ means that God himself has come to earth. Jesus is God in the flesh (Matt. 1:23; John 1:14). He is completely free from sin (Heb. 4:15). In Jesus, God has come in order to redeem us.

What happened to Jesus was, of course, unique to him. But it is analogically related to the new spiritual life that must come to the people of Israel as a whole, and indeed to every individual bound by the shackles of sin:

> The people who walked in darkness
> > have seen a great light;
> those who dwelt in a land of deep darkness,
> > on them has light shone. (Isa. 9:2)

Jesus is fully a human being, but he is fully God as well. Even in his human nature, he has a life from God unlike any other human being. And this uniqueness fits the fact that he is to serve as the origin for new spiritual life to those in spiritual death (Eph. 2:1). The virgin birth was a physical event, but it has symbolic significance: it signifies the necessity of new life radically initiated by God. A virgin

---

[1] Sin is not a physical thing like a virus, passed on biologically in the process of conception and birth. Rather, it is moral and spiritual rebellion against God. We inherit it because Adam was the head of the human race, and represented us when he sinned (Rom. 5:12-21). Jesus is the *last Adam*, a new head of a new humanity. The distinctive character of his virgin conception underscores his unique role.

womb does not have the life of a new human being in it. It is in this respect symbolically "dead." Then God came and created new life, the life of Jesus. This transition from death to life signifies by analogy what must happen to each of us. We must be born again (John 3:3, 5), and so be brought from spiritual death to spiritual life.

Given this significance, we can construct a triangle indicating how the virgin birth points typologically forward to the new life of the resurrection (see fig. 9.1).

Fig. 9.1: Clowney's Triangle for the Virgin Birth

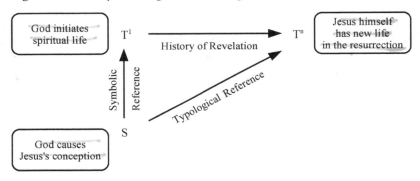

The virgin conception of Jesus also hints at the fact that Jesus is the Son of God in a unique and deep sense, as the Gospel of Luke indicates:

> And the angel answered her, "The Holy Spirit will come upon you, and the power of the Most High will overshadow you; therefore the child to be born will be called holy—*the Son of God.*" (Luke 1:35)

Matthew makes Jesus's Sonship explicit only at a later point, at his baptism. We will therefore defer a discussion of Sonship until then.

Implications for Broader Periods of Time

Through his discussion of the virgin birth, Matthew introduces the theme of God initiating new life. Since this new life is one characteristic of God's kingdom, we expect it to recur in the larger circles of the manifestation of the kingdom. Consider the circle of Jesus's earthly ministry. Jesus gave new spiritual life to people during his entire earthly ministry. This giving of life was further underscored by the instances where he raised people who were dead or near death.

Next, consider Jesus's death and resurrection. The resurrection is the beginning of imperishable life, no longer subject to death (Rom. 6:9–10).

Now what about the spread of the gospel during the book of Acts and later? The gospel brings new life to those to whom it gives new birth:

> . . . you have been born again, not of perishable seed but of imperishable, through the living and abiding *word of God*; . . . And this word is the *good news* that was preached to you. (1 Pet. 1:23, 25)

The giving of new life culminates in the consummation, where all God's people have eternal life in the presence of God forever, by virtue of the new life given to them through Christ (Rev. 21:4; 22:2).

The picture of new eternal life sends us back also to the creation of life in Genesis 1. God made man, and he made provision for the processes leading to the birth of new human beings (Ps. 139:13–16; cf. Gen. 4:1).

We should also ask how the miracle of virgin conception fulfills promises and patterns in the Old Testament. The most obvious connection lies with the passage that Matthew 1:23 cites from Isaiah 7:14. There is much discussion as to the exact significance of Isaiah 7:14. Is Isaiah 7:14 a direct prophecy that describes the birth of the Messiah? Or does it have some connection with a son born during the time of Ahaz (e.g., Isa. 8:3)? If the latter, the son born earlier would still point typologically to the future birth of the Messiah. Whether directly or indirectly, the virgin birth fulfills not only Isaiah 7:14 but also passages concerning the promised offspring of the woman (Gen. 3:15), the offspring of Abraham (Gen. 12:7; 13:15; 17:7; etc.), and the offspring of David (e.g., Mic. 5:2).

We may summarize all these thematic connections with birth and new life in a diagram (figure 9.2).

Fig. 9.2: Circles of Meaning for the Virgin Birth

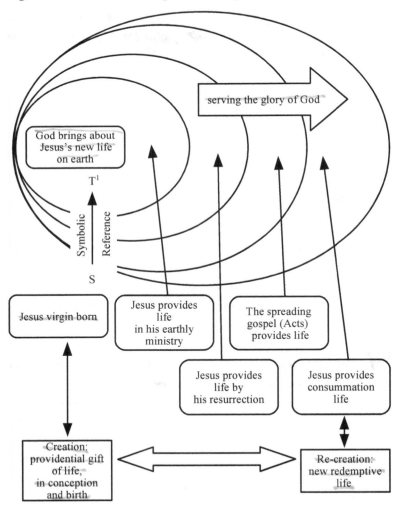

The broad picture of the significance in the virgin birth naturally encourages us to reflect on more specific applications. Certainly one obvious application is for us as readers to see that Jesus is the Messiah, the fulfillment of Old Testament promises, and that he is unique among human beings in the manner of his origin. This special origin testifies to the fact that he is the unique Son of God. But we can also be encouraged to understand that God is pleased to bring radically new life to us through Christ. As usual, we can add to Clowney's triangle a part to indicate application (fig. 9.3).

Fig. 9.3: Clowney's Triangle for the Virgin Birth, with Application

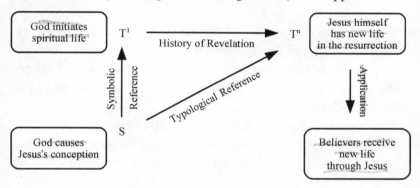

All of these aspects lead us to praising God for his grace, for the gift of his Son, and for the wisdom of his plan worked out in history.

Miraculous Accompaniments to the Virgin Birth

In the Gospel of Matthew some smaller miracles take place in connection with the virgin birth. (1) "An angel of the Lord appeared to him [Joseph] in a dream," encouraging Joseph to take Mary as his wife (Matt. 1:20). (2) A special star appeared to the wise men (Matt. 2:2). (3) The star "went before them until it came to rest over the place where the child was" (Matt. 2:9). (4) The wise men were "warned in a dream not to return to Herod" (Matt. 2:12). (5) "An angel of the Lord appeared to Joseph in a dream," telling him to flee to Egypt (Matt. 2:13). (6) "When Herod died, behold, an angel of the Lord appeared in a dream to Joseph in Egypt," telling Joseph to return to Israel (Matt. 2:19–20). (7) Joseph received another warning "in a dream" and "withdrew to the district of Galilee" (Matt. 2:22).

Each of these miracles belongs to a larger narrative. The larger narrative does not really focus on the miracle itself, as if the miracle were the main point. Rather, each miracle serves to reinforce the sense that God's hand of providence was working in the events that unfolded. Because the miracles serve as a reinforcement, we are not devoting separate chapters to the discussion of each of the small miracles in Matthew. But we may say a few words.

The dream given to Joseph in Matthew 1:20 obviously reinforced the special character of the virgin birth. It also served to provide for Mary and Jesus: Joseph was there as a human protector and a provider of home life. In the events that followed in Matthew 2, Joseph took the initiative in bringing his family down to Egypt and then back to Galilee.

In addition, the dream in Matthew 1:20 encouraged Joseph to undertake the responsibilities of being a legal father to Jesus. This step is important, because it means that Jesus became an heir of the line of kings listed in Matthew 1:6–11. Jesus is the Messiah who fulfills the Old Testament promises concerning a great descendant of David who will be king. Jesus can fulfill these promises because, through Joseph's adoption of Jesus, he belongs to the line of David.[2]

The miracles surrounding the wise men show how God provided protection for Jesus against the murderous designs of Herod. "God will not allow his purpose to be thwarted."[3] In addition, the wise men were Gentiles rather than Jews. So at this early point Matthew underscores the fact that Jesus is the Savior of Gentiles as well as Jews (see also the discussion of the centurion's servant in Matt. 8:5–13; chapter 13 below). The wise men began to fulfill Isaiah's prophecy that Gentiles would bring gifts:

[2] R. T. France, *The Gospel of Matthew* (Grand Rapids, MI: Eerdmans, 2007), 47–48.
[3] Grant R. Osborne, *Matthew* (Grand Rapids, MI: Zondervan, 2010), 92.

> Then you shall see and be radiant;
>> your heart shall thrill and exult,
> because the abundance of the sea shall be turned to you,
>> the wealth of the nations shall come to you.
> A multitude of camels shall cover you,
>> the young camels of Midian and Ephah;
>> all those from Sheba shall come.
> They shall bring *gold* and *frankincense*,
>> and shall bring good news, the praises of the LORD.
>>> (Isa. 60:5–6)

The coming of the wise men is also reminiscent of the coming of the queen of Sheba to visit Solomon. The queen of Sheba was outside the Jewish line. She was therefore a precursor of the coming of the Gentiles. She brought gold and spices (1 Kings 10:10). Psalm 72:8–11 also pictures the messianic king as receiving gifts from the nations.

The coming of the Gentiles takes place in a fuller way after Christ's resurrection, when he issues the Great Commission: "Go therefore and make disciples *of all nations*" (Matt. 28:19). This commission operates on the basis of the completed work of Christ: "All authority in heaven and on earth has been given to me" (v. 18). So the coming of the wise men has a definite link to the climactic fulfillment of God's plan in the crucifixion and the resurrection of Christ.

Applications

All of these small miracles contribute to a picture in which we can appreciate God's plan of redemption as a whole. God controls and plans not only the big pieces in history but the smaller ones as well. And that means those who belong to God through Christ can take courage; their lives are in God's hands:

> Therefore I tell you, do not be anxious about your life, what you will eat or what you will drink, nor about your body, what you will put on. Is not life more than food, and the body more

than clothing? Look at the birds of the air: they neither sow nor reap nor gather into barns, and yet your heavenly Father feeds them. Are you not of more value than they? And which of you by being anxious can add a single hour to his span of life? And why are you anxious about clothing? Consider the lilies of the field, how they grow: they neither toil nor spin, yet I tell you, even Solomon in all his glory was not arrayed like one of these. But if God so clothes the grass of the field, which today is alive and tomorrow is thrown into the oven, will he not much more clothe you, O you of little faith? Therefore do not be anxious, saying, "What shall we eat?" or "What shall we drink?" or "What shall we wear?" For the Gentiles seek after all these things, and your heavenly Father knows that you need them all. But seek first the kingdom of God and his righteousness, and all these things will be added to you. (Matt. 6:25–33)

As we learn to rely on God's providential care, we learn also to praise him rather than to worry: "Do not be anxious" (Matt. 6:31).

10

The Baptism of Jesus
(Matthew 3:13–17)

Next let us consider Matthew's account of the baptism of Jesus. It counts as a miracle because of the voice from heaven and the sign of the dove:

> Then Jesus came from Galilee to the Jordan to John, to be baptized by him. John would have prevented him, saying, "I need to be baptized by you, and do you come to me?" But Jesus answered him, "Let it be so now, for thus it is fitting for us to fulfill all righteousness." Then he consented. And when Jesus was baptized, immediately he went up from the water, and behold, the heavens were opened to him, and he saw the Spirit of God descending like a dove and coming to rest on him; and behold, a voice from heaven said, "This is my beloved Son, with whom I am well pleased." (Matt. 3:13–17)

In the miracle, God proclaimed that Jesus is the unique beloved Son. The sign of the dove indicated that he was filled with the Holy Spirit. In analogy with the work of the Holy Spirit on special leaders in the Old Testament, the Holy Spirit was present with Jesus to empower his public ministry.

How do we understand this empowerment? Jesus is fully God. As God, he is full of all divine wisdom and power, and therefore fully capable for all his work on earth. Yet we also know that God's work is simultaneously the work of the Father, the Son, and the Holy Spirit. So we infer that the Father and the Holy Spirit were both present in Jesus's work as God. In addition, Jesus is fully man. In this respect he is like the judges and prophets and kings whom God raised up in the Old Testament and equipped with his Spirit. The prophets like Moses and Elijah and Elisha did miraculous works that no mere man could accomplish. By analogy, the Holy Spirit came upon Jesus according to his human nature, in order that he might accomplish his work, including the working of miracles.

Son of God

The miracle has as its main point the announcement of the special relation of Christ to the Father, and the special favor of the Father that rests upon him. This special relationship is expressed by the gift of the Holy Spirit. The words from heaven contain allusions to Psalm 2:7 and Isaiah 42:1.[1] It is worthwhile looking at these allusions.

First, consider Psalm 2:7. Psalm 2:7 says, "You are my Son; today I have begotten you." Psalm 2:7 is speaking against the background of David's kingship and God's promise that the final messianic king would be a descendant of David. The Davidic kingship of Old Testament times points forward to the final messianic king. The word "today" in Psalm 2:7 is not identifying the time of Jesus's birth, but the time of his enthronement, as the preceding verse indicates: "I have set my King on Zion, my holy hill" (Ps. 2:6). This focus on enthronement is confirmed by Acts 13:33, which quotes Psalm 2:7 and links it to Christ's resurrection:

---

[1] D. A. Carson, "Matthew," in *The Expositor's Bible Commentary*, rev. ed., ed. Tremper Longman III and David E. Garland, vol. 9 (Grand Rapids, MI: Zondervan, 2010), 137–138. R. T. France also explores a possible allusion to Genesis 22:2 (R. T. France, *The Gospel of Matthew* [Grand Rapids, MI: Eerdmans, 2007], 123). Theologically, Abraham's sacrifice of Isaac points forward to the sacrifice of Christ. So a possible linkage between Matthew 4:17 and Genesis 22:2 makes sense.

. . . this [the promise of God] he has fulfilled to us their children by *raising Jesus*, as also it is written in the second Psalm,

"You are my Son,
today I have begotten you."

Christ's enthronement openly manifested the fact that he is the Son of God: he "was declared to be the Son of God in power according to the Spirit of holiness by his resurrection from the dead, Jesus Christ our Lord" (Rom. 1:4). But he was already the Son of God at his baptism, according to Matthew 3:17. In addition, his Sonship at the time of baptism presupposes his virgin birth. And the virgin birth presupposes his eternal relation to God the Father. He is always the Son, always begotten by the Father. This eternal begetting forms the background for all the later manifestations of his Sonship within time and space. The manifestations in time are always in harmony with who he always is.[2]

Matthew 3:17 also contains an allusion to Isaiah 42:1: "Behold my servant, whom I uphold." Israel was in a sense the Lord's servant, but she repeatedly failed to obey him. Jesus, by contrast, is the true Israel, the true servant, who brings salvation through his death and resurrection, as predicted in the servant passage in Isaiah 52:13–53:12.

The special relation between the Father and the incarnate Christ has its ultimate divine foundation in the eternal fellowship between the Father and the Son through the Holy Spirit. But now this relationship came to be expressed in space and time. The Son became incarnate for the purpose of accomplishing redemption.

The fellowship between the Father and the Son characterized Jesus's entire earthly ministry. It came to expression at the cross in the confession of the centurion, "Truly this was the Son of God!" (Matt. 27:54). Sonship came to climactic expression in Christ's resurrection and ascension. The ascension was implicitly in the background when Christ claimed that "All authority in heaven and on earth has been given to me" (Matt. 28:18). "All authority" is

---

[2] This harmony is one fundamental indication that there is an eternal relationship of Father to Son within the Trinity, and an eternal begetting.

authority from God the Father, so it presupposes the intimate fellowship between the Father and the Son. Christ's promise of being "with you" (Matt. 28:20) is a promise of the universal presence of God, which presupposes the unity of the Father, the Son, and the Holy Spirit. The unity of one God in three persons is further expressed in the formula for baptizing "in the name of the Father and of the Son and of the Holy Spirit (Matt. 28:19). Together, these expressions in Matthew make known the Sonship of the Christ in a manner parallel to the description in Romans 1:3–4:

> . . . concerning his Son, who was descended from David according to the flesh and was declared to be *the Son of God* in power *according to the Spirit of holiness* by his resurrection from the dead, Jesus Christ our Lord, . . .

The Bible calls us to respond to this revelation of Jesus's Sonship by acknowledging him as the Son of God and receiving adoption as sons. When we receive adoption, we respond by praising him and glorifying the name of Christ.

We can summarize the meaning of Christ's Sonship using Clowney's triangle. The vertical leg of the triangle represents the meaning of the miracle of the voice from heaven at the time when it occurs. The voice (the physical manifestation) has the meaning of announcing Sonship. From there we can move forward in our thought to Christ's resurrection and ascension (see fig. 10.1).

Baptismal Identification

In close connection with the voice from heaven we have Jesus's baptism. Matthew records that John the Baptist at first resisted the idea of baptizing Jesus: "John would have prevented him" (Matt. 3:14). John's baptism was explicitly defined as a baptism "for repentance" (v. 11), which involved people "confessing their sins" (v. 6). Somehow John was aware that this kind of baptism did not fit Jesus. He had no sins. But Jesus nevertheless indicated that baptism was not only appropriate, but had the purpose of fulfilling "all righteousness" (v. 15).

Fig. 10.1: Clowney's Triangle for the Voice from Heaven

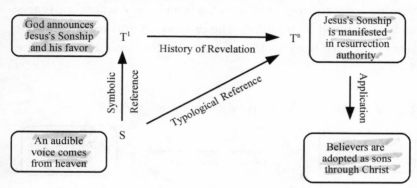

How do we understand this cluster of ideas? Jesus has already been introduced in Matthew 2:15 as the true Israel, the true Son, the obedient Son in contrast to historical Israel's repeated disobedience. By being baptized, he identified with the sinners of Israel who were coming to be baptized. In effect, he was confessing not his own sins (of which he had none) but the sins of Israel, the nation whom he was called to represent. He identified with sinners.

This kind of identification was of course confirmed by his practice of eating and drinking with tax collectors and sinners. That practice in turn pointed forward to the cross, where he would be the sin-bearer for his people: ". . . even as the Son of Man came not to be served but to serve, and to give his life as a *ransom* for many" (Matt. 20:28; see Isa. 53:11–12).

This truth applies to us. We receive forgiveness when we repent and turn to Christ for salvation.

In summary, we can draw a triangle to represent the theme of Jesus's identification with sinners (see fig. 10.2).

Broader Implications of Meaning in Jesus's Sonship and Baptism

As usual, the meanings in this miracle have broader implications. We have already noted that all of Jesus's earthly ministry took place in communion with the Father and with the Spirit. Jesus's Sonship lay at the root of every miracle and every act of forgiveness and every word of teaching. The crucifixion and resurrection of Jesus expressed both his identification with sinners and his divine Sonship.

Fig. 10.2: Clowney's Triangle for the Baptism of Jesus

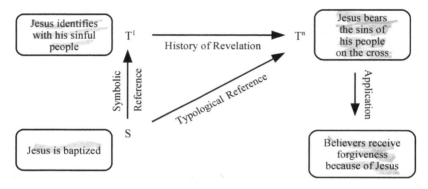

Then, in the book of Acts, Jesus through the power of the Holy Spirit gives to human beings the privilege of sonship. He gives forgiveness of sins on the basis of his substitutionary death. Baptism is the sign of being united to Christ, and therefore implicitly includes the promise of sonship and forgiveness (Matt. 28:19). From the time of Pentecost onward, the gospel of Christ spreads to the nations of the world. People from all nations receive the knowledge and the effects of Jesus's Sonship and sin-bearing. Finally, at the end of the age, God's people will receive perfect sonship and the complete end of sin:

> The one who conquers will have this heritage, and I will be his God and he will be my *son.* (Rev. 21:7)

> But nothing unclean will ever enter it, nor anyone who does what is detestable or false, but only those who are written in the Lamb's book of life. (Rev. 21:27)

They will see his [God's] face, and his name will be on their foreheads. (Rev. 22:4)

As usual, we can summarize the broader implications in a series of broadening circles (fig. 10.3).

Fig. 10.3: Circles of Meaning for the Baptism of Jesus

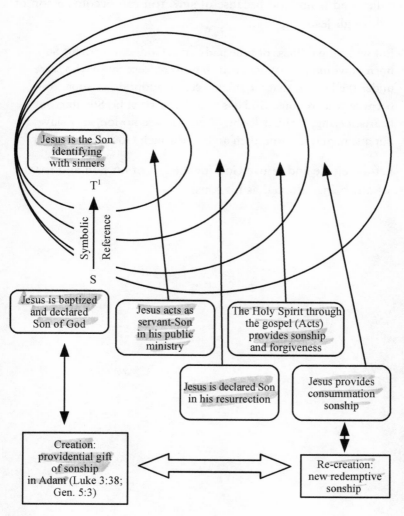

Applications

An understanding of the broader picture again suggests applications. First, we as hearers should take to heart that Jesus is the unique Son of God, fulfilling the plan of God to bring salvation. Salvation is found in Jesus, not in counterfeit alternatives. We can also see the relationship of Jesus's Sonship to our own sonship. Are you alienated from God because of sin? You can become a son of God through Jesus the Son:

> But when the fullness of time had come, God sent forth his Son, born of woman, born under the law, to redeem those who were under the law, so that we might receive adoption as sons. And because you are sons, God has sent the Spirit of his Son into our hearts, crying, "Abba! Father!" So you are no longer a slave, but a son, and if a son, then an heir through God. (Gal. 4:4–7)

Let us rejoice and praise God for the gift of his Son and for the gift of our being adopted as his sons.

11

Many Healings
(Matthew 4:23–25)

Matthew 4:23–25 gives us a summary of the early part of Jesus's public ministry:

> And he went throughout all Galilee, teaching in their syna-gogues and proclaiming the gospel of the kingdom and *healing every disease and every affliction* among the people. So his fame spread throughout all Syria, and they brought him *all the sick, those afflicted with various diseases and pains, those oppressed by demons, epileptics, and paralytics, and he healed them*. And great crowds followed him from Galilee and the Decapolis, and from Jerusalem and Judea, and from beyond the Jordan.

The Significance of Healings

Jesus's ministry included many miracles of healing. Matthew at this early point is providing only a general sketch. His summary emphasizes the extent of Jesus's miracles. He healed "all the sick," by which we are to understand all the sick people who came to him. The following words in the passage underscore the extent of the miracles by mentioning a list of various types of afflictions.

The list includes not only bodily illnesses but also oppression by demons.

What is the theological significance of these miracles? At this early point in Matthew, the text does not provide much direct instruction about the meaning or the theological significance of Jesus's miracles. At a later point Matthew provides a link with the suffering servant of Isaiah 53:

> That evening they brought to him many who were oppressed by demons, and *he cast out the spirits with a word and healed all who were sick.* This was to fulfill what was spoken by the prophet Isaiah: "He took our illnesses and bore our diseases." (Matt. 8:16–17; cf. Isa. 53:4)

According to this passage, Jesus delivered people from demons and from sicknesses. This deliverance has a link with Jesus's bearing our diseases. The full passage in Isaiah 53 uses the language of disease metaphorically to indicate how the coming servant will suffer as a substitute for sin. The fundamental disorder of sin is thus symbolically represented by the subordinate disorders of demon possession and sickness. Deliverance on the physical level symbolizes deliverance on the spiritual level. First Peter 2:24 speaks in a similar way:

> He himself bore our sins in his body on the tree, that we might die to sin and live to righteousness. By his *wounds* you have been *healed*." (cf. Isa. 53:5)

D. A. Carson summarizes, "This means that for Matthew, Jesus' healing miracles pointed beyond themselves to the cross. In this, he is like the evangelist John, whose 'signs' similarly point beyond themselves."[1]

---

[1] D. A. Carson, "Matthew," in *Expositor's Bible Commentary*, rev. ed., ed. Tremper Longman III and David E. Garland, vol. 9 (Grand Rapids, MI: Zondervan, 2010), 244; R. T. France disagrees (R. T. France, *The Gospel of Matthew* [Grand Rapids, MI: Eerdmans, 2007], 322n56), finding in Matthew 8:17 only a reference to physical healing. But the disagreement appears to me to be only over the question of *how directly* Matthew 8:17 invites a connection between healing diseases and Jesus's suffering on the cross. France agrees that elsewhere Matthew builds links between Isaiah 53 and the cross (Matt. 20:28; 26:28; cited in France, *Gospel of Matthew*, 322). When we combine the

We also know that the new heaven and new earth will bring comprehensive deliverance, including both a physical side (the resurrection) and a spiritual side (being free from sin and living freely in the presence of God).[2]

Matthew does not directly introduce all this theological significance within the account of the beginnings of Jesus's ministry in 4:23–25. The narrative is content to give a basic sketch at this early point, and to let the significance unfold later. Matthew does, however, indicate a linkage with the coming of the kingdom of God, which in Old Testament prophecy includes comprehensive deliverance. Jesus was "proclaiming the gospel of the *kingdom*" (v. 23). That is, he announced the good news of the coming of the climactic manifestation of the saving rule of God as king. Together with this announcement came illustrations in the form of healing. The healings revealed God's power at work to bring about deliverance. Thus, the healings were manifestations of the kingdom. The miraculous healings complemented the verbal announcement of the kingdom.

Redemptive Plots

We can also see a broad connection between redemption and healing because of the plot structure of healing. A story about healing presupposes a standard of normality that has been lost. Demon-possessed and sick people are not what they ought to be. The lack of normality illustrates the fact that we are living in a fallen world, alienated from God and subject to curse. The story about healing then moves from the difficulty to its resolution. The person in question is delivered from his or her affliction. This small form of deliverance constitutes a "redemptive plot."[3]

Small deliverances all foreshadow the *great* deliverance, redemption through the cross and resurrection of Christ. In the cross, Christ

---

larger picture in Matthew as a whole with the principle of the unity of the kingdom of God and the forward-pointing character of all the miracles of Jesus, we can see a sign function in all the healing miracles, whether or not such redemptive significance is *directly* in view when Matthew 8:17 quotes from Isaiah 53:4.

[2] Carson, "Matthew," 245.

[3] Vern S. Poythress, *In the Beginning Was the Word: Language—A God-Centered Approach* (Wheaton, IL: Crossway, 2009), chapter 26.

identified with us in our misery—both the misery of sickness and the deeper misery of sin. In the resurrection he triumphed over misery—not only over sickness but also over sadness, tears, mourning, and death itself. The resurrection was also his judicial vindication. It shows his righteousness and God the Father's approval of his obedience. His resurrection counts on our behalf, for our justification: "[he] was delivered up for our trespasses and raised for our justification" (Rom. 4:25). When we are united to Christ, Christ's resurrection is applied to us, and we receive definitive healing from sin and guilt. We also look forward to the consummation, when the resurrection of the body results in final deliverance from all sin and all attacks by Satan and his hosts.

We can thus draw a triangle to represent the significance of physical healing (fig. 11.1).

Fig. 11.1: Clowney's Triangle for Many Healings

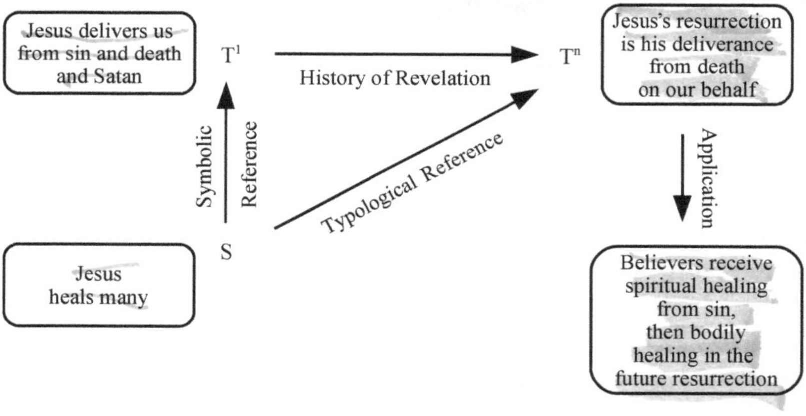

The instances of healing point forward to the great healing in the resurrection of Christ.

Application of Redemption

Miracles of healing also imply that redemption can be applied to us in this age. Christ lives forever as the Savior. His power is available to all who call on him. Thus the instances of healing in Matthew can be used in sermons. The modern proclaimer of the gospel announces that the saving reign of God has begun through Jesus's work. He invites all who are sick or oppressed by Satan to come. "Come and be healed." The healing is first of all the healing from sin and spiritual death. Jesus's resurrection, says the preacher, reaches human need even more deeply and decisively than did the healing miracles that touched bodily needs. Jesus will bring an answer to every bodily need at the time of the consummation. Until then, we may sometimes experience bodily healing, and sometimes not, according to what God wills.[4]

---

[4] The "prosperity gospel," all too common among some preachers today, falsifies the true gospel when it says that God always wants Christians to be healthy and wealthy *in this life*. It eliminates Christian suffering, about which the New Testament speaks clearly (John 16:33; Acts 14:22; Phil. 3:10; 1 Thess. 3:3–4; 1 Pet. 1:6–7; 4:12–13). Prosperity teaching tells naive people what they want to hear rather than what the Bible teaches. It also "jumps the gun" by promising in this life what belongs to the next: followers of Christ will indeed inherit the world itself and perfection in the body, but only at the consummation.

12

Cleansing a Leper
(Matthew 8:1–4)

Matthew 8–9 records how the gospel of the kingdom of God and the power of the kingdom expand in their reach. The section begins with a miracle where Jesus heals a man with leprosy:

> When he came down from the mountain, great crowds followed him. And behold, a leper came to him and knelt before him, saying, "Lord, if you will, you can make me clean." And Jesus stretched out his hand and touched him, saying, "I will; be clean." And immediately his leprosy *was cleansed*. And Jesus said to him, "See that you say nothing to anyone, but go, show yourself to the priest and offer the gift that Moses commanded, for a proof to them." (Matt. 8:1–4)

In this miracle Jesus acts with the power of the kingdom of God to reach out and touch a person on the margins of society.

The Significance of Leprosy

What is the significance of this healing? We should clarify that the term *leprosy* in the context of the Bible designates a spectrum of skin diseases—it is not to be identified with the modern usage in which it refers only to Hansen's disease. In the Old Testament ceremonial law leprosy had a particular role. The person who had it was "unclean," and was disqualified from approaching the presence of God in the tabernacle or the temple. He had to live away from other people (Lev. 13:45–46). Uncleanness was not in itself a sin. But it was a *symbol* for sin, as we see from the way it represented a barrier to approaching the symbolic presence of God in the temple. So when Jesus healed the leper, the healing was symbolic for healing from sin.

Moreover, the Jews understood that touching a leper would communicate uncleanness from one person to another (Lev. 5:3). Jesus touched the leper (Matt. 8:3), which was a startling act within that culture. People would expect that uncleanness would be communicated from the leper to Jesus. Instead, by Jesus's power, *cleanness* was communicated from Jesus to the leper. But still, touching the leper was a sign of identification. Just as the baptism of Jesus signified his identification with the sins of the people, so here his touch indicated his willingness to identify with leprosy, which symbolized sin. His identification with sin at this point anticipated and foreshadowed his identification with sin when he became our sin-bearer on the cross and was forsaken by God (Matt. 27:45–46). Jesus did not literally take the uncleanness of the leper on himself. But he did take our sins on himself, by bearing their punishment: "He himself bore our sins in his body on the tree, that we might die to sin and live to righteousness. By his wounds you have been healed" (1 Pet. 2:24; cf. Isa. 53:4–5).

The leper was a despised and marginalized person within Jewish society. By interacting with the leper, Jesus showed that he has compassion on those who are despised and are suffering. He reached out physically to the leper to touch him. He also reached out metaphorically to heal him. Both aspects signify that Jesus gives blessings to people who do not deserve it. That is the meaning of God's grace—that we receive the opposite of what we deserve. At the deepest level, we are all undeserving and sinful. Salvation is a gift from God through Jesus, not a reward for our good behavior.

The Role of Faith

We should also note the leper's expression of faith: "Lord, if you will, you can make me clean" (Matt. 8:2). The leper expressed confidence in Jesus's power to heal. In the leper's mind, the only question was whether Jesus was willing. If the leper was going to be healed, Jesus must have mercy; the leper could not claim any right or worthiness. This response by the leper offers a picture of the role of faith in salvation. We must place our trust in Jesus as the one who has power to save. And in doing so, we admit that we cannot claim salvation as a right, on the basis of something in ourselves.

A Testimony

Why did Jesus tell the cleansed leper to show himself to the priest? Matthew does not give a further explanation, but two reasons lie close at hand.

First, the process of going to the priest was the proper procedure, as prescribed in the Mosaic law (Lev. 14:1–32). This piece of ceremonial law was still in force during the time before Jesus's resurrection, while the kingdom of God was just beginning to dawn. Through this procedure the man would be officially pronounced clean, and he could be reintegrated into society and could regain access to the temple. This reintegration symbolized the deeper spiritual reality of having sins forgiven and being reconciled both to fellow human beings (society) and to God (symbolized by the temple).

Second, Jesus's instructions to the cleansed leper pointed back to the passages in the Mosaic law regarding leprosy (Leviticus 13–14). By pointing to these passages, Jesus drew attention to all of the symbolism pertaining to leprosy. By evoking the symbolism, he was also telling both the leper and all who observed the miracle not to confine their observation to the obvious fact of the healing of a disease, but to see its symbolic significance, when interpreted against the background of the symbolism of the law of Moses. In this way Jesus encouraged people to understand the significance of the miracle as a sign of redemption from *sin*.

We can summarize the significance of the healing using Clowney's triangle (see fig. 12.1).

Fig. 12.1: Clowney's Triangle for the Cleansing of a Leper

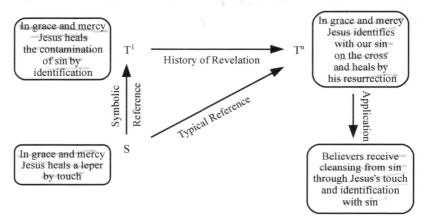

Application of Redemption

The healing of the leper is connected to the central acts of redemption. And these central acts are in turn related to us, because they apply to those in union with Christ. Hence, we can understand the appropriateness of a preaching application. Each of us by nature is a kind of spiritual leper. Sin disqualifies us from communion both with God and with man. Through the message in Matthew, God shows us that each of us must appeal to the living Christ for help. "Lord, if you will, you can make me clean" (Matt. 8:2). We are to have faith in Christ. And what will Christ do in response? He will touch us spiritually, taking away our sin through his substitutionary work. And he will make us clean: he says, "I will; be clean" (v. 3). It is a glorious picture of redemption being applied to an individual. The picture communicates God's plan effectively because of the intrinsic, organic relationships among several realities: leprosy, the miracle in Matthew 8, Jesus's work on the cross, and the purpose of God to apply his work through the Holy Spirit to those who believe.

13

The Centurion's Servant
(Matthew 8:5–13)

In the miracle with the centurion's servant, Jesus shows how the power of God's kingdom reaches out to the Gentile world. Here is the story, in Matthew 8:5–13:

When he entered Capernaum, a centurion came forward to him, appealing to him, "Lord, my servant is lying paralyzed at home, suffering terribly." And he said to him, "I will come and heal him." But the centurion replied, "Lord, I am not worthy to have you come under my roof, but only say the word, and my servant will be healed. For I too am a man under authority, with soldiers under me. And I say to one, 'Go,' and he goes, and to another, 'Come,' and he comes, and to my servant, 'Do this,' and he does it." When Jesus heard this, he marveled and said to those who followed him, "Truly, I tell you, with no one in Israel have I found such faith. I tell you, many will come from east and west and recline at table with Abraham, Isaac, and Jacob in the kingdom of heaven, while the sons of the kingdom will be thrown into the outer darkness. In that place there will be weeping and gnashing of teeth." And to the centurion Jesus said, "Go; let it be done for you as you have believed." And the servant was healed at that very moment.

The Gospel to Gentiles

This miracle shows some distinctive features about the kingdom of God. The most obvious distinctive about this miracle is that the centurion is a Gentile, not a Jew. Jesus noted the contrast between the centurion's faith and what was true for Israel:

> Truly, I tell you, with no one *in Israel* have I found such faith. I tell you, many will come from *east and west* and recline at table with Abraham, Isaac, and Jacob in the kingdom of heaven, *while the sons of the kingdom* will be thrown into the outer darkness. (Matt. 8:10–12)

Jesus raised the issue of who would participate in the kingdom of God and "recline at table" with the patriarchs "in the kingdom of heaven." The centurion's faith indicated that he and those like him would participate, though they were Gentiles. The centurion and his servant *did* participate in the effects of God's power when Jesus healed the servant. But in addition, this miracle like the others points forward to the stages when the kingdom of God expands and deepens even further.

The crucifixion and the resurrection of Christ are the climax. Those who participate in the kingdom of God are the same as those who are united with Christ and who participate in the benefits of his work on the cross. Gentiles and Jews can participate by faith, as the book of Acts makes clear and as Matthew makes clear by the Great Commission:

> And Jesus came and said to them, "All authority in heaven and *on earth* has been given to me. Go therefore and make *disciples of all nations*, baptizing them in the name of the Father and of the Son and of the Holy Spirit, . . . (Matt. 28:18–19)

Like the leper in Matthew 8:1–4, the centurion was a person at the margins of Jewish society. He was a Gentile; socially, he was completely outside the circle of Judaism. By reaching out to him, Jesus showed that his saving compassion extends beyond the circle of Judaism.

Healing at a Distance

When Jesus healed at a distance, it showed that the kingdom of God was breaking through barriers of space. As the centurion recognized (Matt. 8:8–9), Jesus had supernatural authority. By that authority he could exert the power of the kingdom of God over the centurion's servant, far from his earthly location at Capernaum. This authority is a characteristic of the kingdom of God as a whole. Consequently, the further development of the growth of the kingdom, through Jesus's death and resurrection, expresses the same principle. Jesus's death and resurrection have the power to change people who are distant from Jerusalem in space, and to change people who are also distant in time, throughout all generations.

After Jesus's resurrection, the gospel and the power of the kingdom begin in Acts to spread through the entire world, overcoming the barriers of space. The spread of the gospel takes place under Jesus's universal authority: "All authority in heaven and on earth has been given to me" (Matt. 28:18). This authority is a fuller expression of the principle that became visible in the miracle with the centurion's servant. Jesus's ascension to heaven implies that physically he is absent from the earth, but spiritually his presence can extend to the end of the earth (Acts 1:8) through the Holy Spirit.

Healing as a Sign of Restoration

As usual, healing on a physical plane symbolizes the comprehensive healing that God has promised in the Old Testament as the fruit of his coming work of salvation. The servant of the centurion is described as "lying paralyzed at home, suffering terribly" (Matt. 8:6). Jesus replaced paralysis with freedom of movement, and terrible suffering with relief from suffering. Matthew later shows the connection between physical paralysis and the forgiveness of sin (9:2, 5). Sin, we see, is a kind of spiritual paralysis; it disables human beings. Human suffering is not always directly due to individual sin, but still it is an emblem or sign of the results that follow from sin. Christ suffered in order to deliver us from the suffering produced by sin. His resurrection is the beginning point for being freed from sin and suffering.

Clowney's Triangle Applied to the Centurion's Servant

We may summarize the significance of this healing miracle using Clowney's triangle (fig. 13.1).

Fig. 13.1: Clowney's Triangle for the Healing of the Centurion's Servant

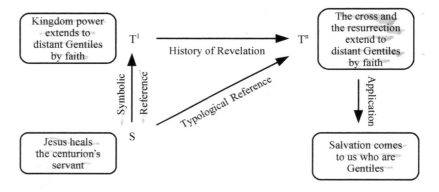

Application

We can see how this miracle has organic implications for application. Are you a "far-off" Gentile, who in misery sees himself as hopelessly beyond the reach of God's favor? Or are you a "near-by" Jew? Both Gentiles and Jews can receive a place in God's kingdom, through faith in Jesus. Are you paralyzed by sin, and suffering terribly in spirit? Appeal to Jesus, who lives and reigns in heaven today. Does Jesus have authority to heal at a distance, from heaven itself? Will he? Have faith in him—the same Jesus who responded to the centurion in his unworthiness.

14

Peter's Mother-in-Law
(Matthew 8:14–17)

The kingdom of God extends in power to people's relatives and neighbors. We see it happening in Matthew 8:14–17:

> And when Jesus entered Peter's house, he saw his mother-in-law lying sick with a fever. He touched her hand, and the fever left her, and she rose and began to serve him. That evening they brought to him many who were oppressed by demons, and he cast out the spirits with a word and healed all who were sick. This was to fulfill what was spoken by the prophet Isaiah: "He took our illnesses and bore our diseases."

The Significance of Healing

We commented earlier (chapter 11) on Matthew's quotation from Isaiah: "He took our illnesses and bore our diseases" (Matt. 8:17; cf. Isa. 53:4). When we take this quotation in the context of all of Isaiah 53, it underscores the connection between Jesus healing diseases and the more radical "healing" through his suffering on the cross.

This miracle about the healing of Peter's mother-in-law shows how the kingdom of God may work through social relationships.

Jesus healed Peter's mother-in-law partly because of the circumstances. He was in the house of Peter. He saw Peter's mother-in-law. This was all partly because of the mother-in-law's relation to Peter. And then healing extended to the larger neighborhood, as people spread the news through the social network.

The most fundamental "social" relation was the relation between the disciples and the Lord himself. This relationship displays in shadowy, seed form what takes place through spiritual union with Christ. The blessings of God's saving reign come through Christ to those in vital spiritual union with Christ. This union comes especially into focus in union with the death and resurrection of Christ (Romans 6). In Christ we receive all the benefits of salvation (Eph. 1:3). And God uses those people who are in union with Christ to spread the good news to others, some of whom in turn come to be united with Christ.

It is also worth noting that Peter's mother-in-law, as a woman, had a social position inferior to that of Jewish men. Jesus's compassion and his salvation extend to women and children, not just to men; and they extend to the lowly, not just to the prominent.

When Peter's mother-in-law was healed, "she rose and began to serve him" (Matt. 8:15). This immediate renewal of energy on her part was one phase of the miracle. In normal circumstances, a fever wears down the body, so that a person has no energy immediately after the fever is over. By contrast, Peter's mother-in-law had full physical energy immediately after the fever left. This renewal of energy came from God, through the person of Jesus. It therefore symbolizes the giving of spiritual energy through the coming of the kingdom of God. That spiritual energy is climactically manifested in Jesus's resurrection from the dead. His resurrection is not like a slow and fitful recovery from a near-death illness. Rather, he has the full power of resurrection life immediately. We may infer that the same principle holds for those included in the kingdom of God through faith in him. They rise and begin to serve him, through the power of the Holy Spirit. Their service is a form of praise, giving glory to God.

Clowney's Triangle for the Healing of Peter's Mother-in-Law

Once again we may summarize our observations using Clowney's triangle for typology (fig. 14.1).

Fig. 14.1: Clowney's Triangle for the Healing of Peter's Mother-in-Law

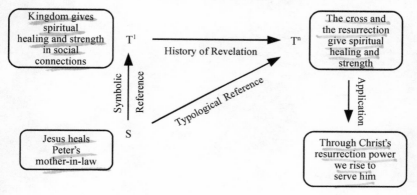

15

Calming a Storm
(Matthew 8:23–27)

The power of the kingdom of God extends to the world of nature. Jesus has authority over the storm and the waves, as indicated in Matthew's narrative:

> And when he got into the boat, his disciples followed him. And behold, there arose a great storm on the sea, so that the boat was being swamped by the waves; but he was asleep. And they went and woke him, saying, "Save us, Lord; we are perishing." And he said to them, "Why are you afraid, O you of little faith?" Then he rose and rebuked *the winds and the sea*, and there was a great calm. And the men marveled, saying, "What sort of man is this, that even winds and sea obey him?" (Matt. 8:23–27)

At the conclusion of the narrative, the disciples asked, "What sort of man is this, . . . ?" In the light of the rest of the Gospel of Matthew, the answer is that Jesus is indeed a man, but he is also the Son of God who shares the character of God along with the Father and the Holy Spirit (Matt. 28:19). Only God can control the winds and the sea (Ps. 107:23–32).[1] This miracle testifies to Jesus's divine nature.

---

[1] Satan was involved in the wind that struck the house where Job's sons and daughters were. But this took place only by God's permission (Job 1:12, 21).

The Significance of Power

So, like all the miracles, this miracle is a display of *power*. But having seen how miracles serve as signs of redemption, we can ask whether this one does as well. Does the calming of the sea merely show raw power, and nothing else?

The occasion is significant. The disciples were in the boat along with Jesus. The boat was "being swamped by the waves." The disciples feared that the boat and all who were in it were about to go down. They said, "*Save* us, Lord; we are *perishing*." They asked to be saved from "perishing," from physically dying by drowning in the sea. The narrative brings up the fundamental issue of life and death.

The larger context of redemptive history is a context in which the issue of life and death is of great importance. Ever since the fall into sin, all mankind has been subject to the penalty of death. We all die eventually. The storm presents an intense and dramatic form of the threat of death. But in a broader way the threat of death is always there. Its threat belongs to the existential situation that confronts us all. We also know, from the discussion in Genesis 3 about the fall, that physical death is emblematic of the spiritual death of separation from God.

So Jesus's miracle is not *merely* an exhibition of his power. It is also an exhibition of his power to *save* people. He works the miracle on behalf of people who are on the point of sinking into death.

The Symbolism of Water

The watery situation is an effective picture of the threat of death. Human beings cannot live in water—even a good swimmer will eventually drown if he cannot reach land, and stormy water is more threatening for both swimmers and nonswimmers. Sinking into the water is like sinking into the grave, into the underworld. Accordingly, Jonah's experience of going down into the sea and being underwater in the belly of the fish functions as a metaphorical death-and-resurrection experience for Jonah. Jesus accordingly referred to Jonah in prophesying his own literal death and resurrection:

> For just as Jonah was three days and three nights in the belly of the great fish, so will the Son of Man be three days and three nights in the heart of the earth. (Matt. 12:40)

More broadly, the Bible often uses the symbolism of waters to describe the threat of death:

> Save me, O God!
>> For the *waters* have come up to my neck.
> I sink in deep mire,
>> where there is no foothold;
> I have come into *deep waters*,
>> and the *flood* sweeps over me. (Ps. 69:1–2)

Thus, when Jesus rescued the disciples from the storm, this rescue pointed beyond the waters to the larger issue of death. The miracle symbolizes Jesus rescuing disciples from death in a permanent way. And the death from which he rescues them encompasses not only physical death but spiritual death as well. Through him we come to be united in fellowship with God, who is the source of true life, eternal life.

This theme of rescue from death has a connection with Jesus's own encounter with death and life, in his death and resurrection. For our sake, Jesus suffered death. And now that he has been raised, his new life belongs not only to him personally but also to us who believe in him. He was "delivered up for our trespasses and raised for our justification" (Rom. 4:25). He was delivered up to suffering and death because our trespasses deserved death. He was raised to life in order that new life might come to us (Rom. 6:3–4). In that new life we serve him with praise and give glory to God.

Clowney's Triangle for Calming the Storm

We may summarize the significance of this miracle using Clowney's triangle (fig. 15.1).

Fig. 15.1: Clowney's Triangle for the Calming of the Storm

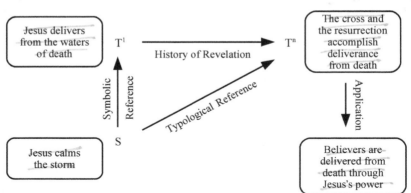

Application

An application to salvation from sin is natural and is organically related to the story, because, within the context of Matthew, the story is related to the accomplishment of salvation in the death and resurrection of Christ. And by God's design, his death and resurrection took place not only for him but also for the benefit of those who believe in him and who are united to him.

I have heard some people make fun of preachers who use this story to talk about the "storms of life." The critics correctly observe that the story is about a storm on the sea of Galilee during Jesus's earthly life, not about metaphorical "storms" of troubles and distresses that afflict modern people. Well, yes, the story is about a real event that took place back then and there. Strictly speaking, the event has never been repeated.

But it is also true that a story like this one has a larger significance, because the kingdom of God and the saving work of God through Christ have an organic unity. The principle of salvation from sin and death belongs to the kingdom of God as a whole. Small-scale troubles and distresses in the lives of ordinary people are not on the same level as an immediate and pressing threat of bodily death. But such distresses still represent threats. In response to threats, we call on God through Christ to deliver us.

When we receive a small-scale deliverance, it is one small step belonging to the comprehensive deliverance that salvation represents. Salvation is holistic. It is proper to keep our focus on the central work of Christ, and the central deliverance from sin and death. It is also proper to understand that the central work of Christ has implications for our lives every day:

> . . . always carrying in the body the *death* of Jesus, so that the *life* of Jesus may also be manifested in our bodies. For we who live are always being given over to *death* for Jesus' sake, so that the *life* of Jesus also may be manifested in our mortal flesh. So *death* is at work in us, but *life* in you. (2 Cor. 4:10–12)

As we grow in appreciating these implications, we should be growing also in honoring God and praising his name.

16

The Gadarene Demoniacs
(Matthew 8:28–34)

In the story of the Gadarene demoniacs[1] we see the kingdom of God extending to encompass within its power people whose humanity has been wrecked by the presence of demons:

> And when he came to the other side, to the country of the Gadarenes,[2] two demon-possessed men met him, coming out of the tombs, so fierce that no one could pass that way. And behold, they cried out, "What have you to do with us, O Son of God? Have you come here to torment us before the time?" Now a herd of many pigs was feeding at some distance from them. And the demons begged him, saying, "If you cast us out, send us away into the herd of pigs." And he said to them, "Go." So they came out and went into the pigs, and behold, the whole

---

[1] Mark (5:1–20) and Luke (8:26–39) each have a similar story, but mention only one demoniac. The easiest and most likely explanation, in my opinion, is that there were two, but Mark and Luke mention only one, who was more prominent (Vern S. Poythress, *Inerrancy and the Gospels: A God-Centered Approach to the Challenges of Harmonization* [Wheaton, IL: Crossway, 2012], 56–57).

[2] The ancient manuscripts of this passage differ in spelling: Gadarenes, Gerasenes, Gergesenes, or Gazarenes. Gazarene is probably an alternate spelling of Gadarene. Gerasene and Gergesene may be alternate spellings of the same place name. Gadara and Gerasa are both towns on the east side of the Sea of Galilee. Gadara is most likely the original reading in Matthew. See Bruce M. Metzger, *A Textual Commentary on the Greek New Testament*, 2nd ed. (London/New York: United Bible Societies, 1994), 18–19; Craig Blomberg, *The Historical Reliability of the Gospels*, 2nd ed. (Downers Grove, IL: InterVarsity Press; Nottingham, England: Apollos, 2007), 192.

herd rushed down the steep bank into the sea and drowned in the waters. The herdsmen fled, and going into the city they told everything, especially what had happened to the demon-possessed men. And behold, all the city came out to meet Jesus, and when they saw him, they begged him to leave their region. (Matt. 8:28–34)

The story shows the desperate state of the demoniacs. They were "fierce," like beasts. They came "out of the tombs," reminding us of death and the near-destruction of the humanity of the two men. Jesus delivered them from their affliction, and in addition accomplished judgment on the demons. The pigs perished in the sea, symbolizing how the destiny of demons is for them to be judged by God and consigned to hell.

Salvific Significance

How do we react to this story? Some people, affected by modern secularism or materialism, do not believe in demons. In their opinion, demons belong to an era of "primitive superstition" that they have left behind. But why do they believe that demons do not exist? Usually, it is because they have absorbed the belief from others around them who believe the same thing. But if so, this belief has no more substantial backing than the "superstitions" that they associate with other times, for in other times as well, many people just went along with what other people around them believed.

Most modern science focuses on the material aspect of reality. But a focus on the material cannot prove that what is material is the only thing that exists. We are better off if we recognize that all human knowledge of the spirit world is limited. And then the questions about demons depend on the questions about whether the Bible is a trustworthy source of knowledge, and whether Jesus knew what he was doing when he dealt with the demonic realm. We have already indicated why we should have confidence both in Jesus and in the Bible as the word of God. So the world of demons is real. Demons are powerful spiritual beings, and they may oppress people in ways that distort or degrade their human potential.[3]

The key role of the demons in the story about the Gadarene demoniacs leads to reflections on the way in which the coming of the kingdom of God saves people from demonic oppression and accusation as well as from sin. The kingdom of God opposes the kingdom of evil, which has Satan as its head. Satan tries to control people through more than one method. Demonic oppression, such as we see with the Gadarene demoniacs, is only one form. In addition, Satan tempts people to do evil. And the Bible indicates that everyone who is in rebellion against God belongs to Satan's kingdom in a broad sense:

> We know that everyone who has been born of God does not keep on sinning, but he who was born of God protects him, and the evil one does not touch him.
>
> We know that we are from God, and the whole world lies in the power of the evil one. (1 John 5:18–19)

The decisive defeat of Satan and his hosts consists in delivering not merely people who suffer the intense oppression of demonization, but all who are attacked by demons. Jesus's resistance to Satanic temptation in the wilderness foreshadows his climactic triumph over Satan and evil in his crucifixion and resurrection. The coming of the kingdom of God is the defeat and undoing of the kingdom of Satan:

> And if Satan casts out Satan, he is divided against himself. How then will his kingdom stand? And if I cast out demons by Beelzebul, by whom do your sons cast them out? Therefore they will be your judges. But if it is by the Spirit of God that I cast out demons, then the kingdom of God has come upon you. Or how can someone enter a strong man's house and plunder his goods, unless he first binds the strong man? Then indeed he may plunder his house. (Matt. 12:26–29)

---

[3] In fact, the disbelief in demons characterizing the Western world is an instance of cultural chauvinism and parochialism. See, e.g., John L. Nevius, *Demon Possession and Allied Themes: Being an Inductive Study of Phenomena of Our Own Times* (Chicago: F. H. Revell, 1896).

In the comparison that Jesus used, Satan is "the strong man." The one who binds him must be Jesus himself. The fact that Jesus cast out demons demonstrated not only that Jesus and Satan were on opposing sides, but that Jesus had *already* bound the strong man in a fundamental sense. Yet a more complete triumph over Satan was yet to come. Satan received defeat when Jesus received "all authority" (Matt. 28:18). A similar point is made in Colossians 2:15:

> He disarmed the rulers and authorities and put them to open shame, by triumphing over them in him.

The point at which the rulers and authorities were "disarmed" was the cross: "This [the record of debt] he set aside, nailing it to the cross" (Col. 2:14). The triumph over Satan in Jesus's exorcisms foreshadowed the time when he defeated Satan on the cross.

Since Jesus has defeated Satan in his crucifixion and resurrection, he is able to deliver those who are held captive to sin and evil:

> He has delivered us from the domain of darkness and transferred us to the kingdom of his beloved Son, in whom we have redemption, the forgiveness of sins. (Col. 1:13–14)

> Since therefore the children share in flesh and blood, he himself likewise partook of the same things, that through death he might destroy the one who has the power of death, that is, the devil, and deliver all those who through fear of death were subject to lifelong slavery. (Heb. 2:14–15)

When reading the story of the Gadarene demoniacs, people sometimes worry about the poor pigs. The demons went into the pigs, who then rushed down the steep bank and drowned in the sea (Matt. 8:32). But human beings are of greater value than pigs. (In addition, even if the pigs had survived this episode, they would eventually have been eaten!) The demoniacs were delivered, and that is at the center of the story.

We must also reckon with the fact that, in Old Testament symbolism, pigs are unclean animals, and that uncleanness symbolizes sin and death. The sea is also a suitable symbol for the final abyss of hell, to which demons will eventually go. The demons did not go to hell at this point in time. But the fact that they went down to the sea, into an *abyss*, symbolized in a striking way that they were defeated by Jesus. This initial defeat anticipates the final defeat that they will experience on the day of judgment (Rev. 20:10).

Summary with Clowney's Triangle

Because the kingdom of God and the kingdom of Satan are so obviously opposed to each other, it is comparatively easy to summarize the significance of this miracle using Clowney's triangle (fig. 16.1).

Fig. 16.1: Clowney's Triangle for the Deliverance of the Gadarene Demoniacs

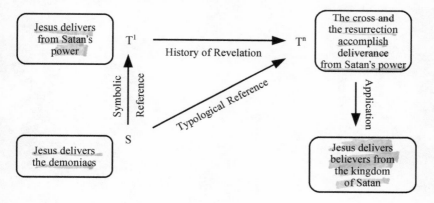

Application

The demoniacs represent an extreme case of human beings dominated by Satanic power. But as we saw from 1 John 5:19, the whole world of sinful human beings is under the power of the Devil. Everyone has had his humanity corrupted and degraded by sin and Satan. We need deliverance. Jesus in the only one who can bring such deliverance, through his cross and resurrection. So the passage summons us to come to Jesus for deliverance. Then we should also praise him for our deliverance, and spread the news of deliverance to others:

"Go home to your friends and tell them how much the Lord has done for you, and how he has had mercy on you." And he went away and began to proclaim in the Decapolis how much Jesus had done for him, and everyone marveled. (Mark 5:19–20)

"Everyone marveled," it says. This marveling points toward the goal of glorifying God. We should give praise to God as we marvel over what Jesus did for the Gadarene demoniacs and what he continues to do in delivering people from the power of Satan. He delivers people from then until now and into the future, until he returns.

17

Healing a Paralytic
(Matthew 9:1–8)

Next we consider the healing of the paralytic in Matthew 9:1–8:

> And getting into a boat he crossed over and came to his own
> city. And behold, some people brought to him a paralytic, lying
> on a bed. And when Jesus saw their faith, he said to the para-
> lytic, "Take heart, my son; your sins are forgiven." And behold,
> some of the scribes said to themselves, "This man is blasphem-
> ing." But Jesus, knowing their thoughts, said, "Why do you
> think evil in your hearts? For which is easier, to say, 'Your sins
> are forgiven,' or to say, 'Rise and walk'? But that you may know
> that the Son of Man has authority on earth to forgive sins"—
> he then said to the paralytic—"Rise, pick up your bed and go
> home." And he rose and went home. When the crowds saw it,
> they were afraid, and they glorified God, who had given such
> authority to men.

The kingdom of God encompasses not simply deliverance from
bodily affliction but the forgiveness of sins.

The Significance of Healing the Paralytic
In this case Jesus did not heal the man right away. Instead, he first
pronounced that the man's sins were forgiven (v. 2). This response

is striking because the people who brought the paralytic were obviously hoping for physical healing. Why did Jesus not respond in a straightforward way? Jesus's response is also striking because it stirred up opposition from the scribes. They said, "This man is blaspheming" (v. 3). Why did Jesus choose to provoke this kind of opposition, when it looks as though he could have avoided it by simply confining himself to healing and making no pronouncement about forgiveness?

But once we ask the question, a partial answer suggests itself. Jesus was interested in more than physical healing. He was genuinely concerned for the man to understand that his sins were forgiven. The narrative does not tell us anything more about the man. We do not know whether his paralysis was a direct or indirect consequence of particular sins, or whether it was only another instance of human suffering that characterizes this fallen world. Since the narrative does not supply any detail, it invites us to focus all the more on what it does indicate, namely that "the Son of Man has authority on earth to forgive sins" (v. 6). If so, his authority was one sign that the kingdom of God was dawning, and that one feature of the kingdom was the accomplishment of forgiveness.

So the disorders of the body, and paralysis in particular, can symbolize the disorders of the soul, namely sin. If we press the comparison, we might even say that sin is a kind of paralysis of the soul. It prevents us from moving and acting as we were originally created to do, by acting to love and serve God. The healing of the body corresponds to the healing of the soul, and this miracle makes the symbolic correspondence explicit.

Responses to the Miracle

The response from the crowd is also significant: "When the crowds saw it, they were afraid, and they glorified God, who had given such authority to men" (v. 8). Their fear may have had mixed causes or motives. They might have been reverentially fearing God; they might have been showing self-centered fear, in wanting to protect themselves from power that might be exercised in a way that would threaten their desires. Or their fear might have been for a mixture of reasons. Their response invites the reader also to respond, in reverential fear and in giving glory to God.

The crowds recognized that Jesus had authority: ". . . who had given such authority to men." But their recognition at this point was partial. They saw the goodness of God. And they saw the way in which he had drawn near to human beings not only by forgiving sins but by giving "such authority to men." The last expression emphasizes that God has drawn near to human beings, by giving authority "to men." But, strikingly, the people did not say, ". . . to Jesus" or ". . . to the Son of Man." Their response, ". . . to men," was surely more vague than it should have been. They indicated in this response that they had not yet come to a settled conviction as to what role Jesus as an individual was playing in God's work among them.

Moreover, the crowds apparently had not yet made the inferences that the scribes among them made, as revealed by the parallel passages in Mark and Luke: "Who can forgive sins but God alone?" (Mark 2:7; Luke 5:21). By forgiving sins, Jesus revealed his divine nature. The crowds considered him to be a *man*; and they were of course right—he was fully human. They had not yet realized that he is divine, the Son of God, sharing the name of God with the Father and the Spirit (Matt. 28:19). The response from the crowd also raises a pointed question for every reader: "What do *you* think? Who is Jesus? And does he have power to forgive your sins?"

We should also reckon with the negative response from the scribes. Their opposition was part of a broader pattern of opposition to Jesus that eventually led to the crucifixion. The negative link to the crucifixion through the theme of opposition complements the positive link through the theme of forgiveness of sins. Forgiveness of sins was definitively established through Jesus's identification with sin on the cross and through Jesus giving "his life as a ransom for many" (Matt. 20:28).

Clowney's Triangle Applied to the Paralytic

We may summarize the significance of the healing of the paralytic using Clowney's triangle (fig. 17.1).

Fig. 17.1: Clowney's Triangle for the Healing of the Paralytic

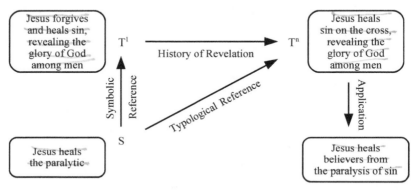

Application

The reality of the application of Jesus's redemptive work within this age leads naturally to recognizing an organic connection between this story and modern application. Jesus is alive forever at the right hand of God. You may come to him because you earnestly or desperately desire to be healed—perhaps from some physical disease, perhaps from some spiritual or mental or psychological paralysis or disability. But underneath, perhaps not recognized, you have a deeper and more desperate need: to have your sins forgiven, to be reconciled to God, and to establish a personal relationship with God in which God blesses you. Jesus may determine to heal your physical trouble, as he chooses. But when you meet him, you must reckon above all with the issue of sin. He offers you forgiveness on the basis of his substitutionary work on the cross.

We should also recognize that, through the unifying character of the kingdom of God, significance belongs to the people who brought the paralytic to Jesus. The text says that "Jesus saw *their* faith" (Matt. 9:2), not the faith of the paralytic. This picture should encourage those who in our own age are endeavoring to bring others to Jesus.

We try to bring people to Jesus in a spiritual sense. Jesus can forgive the sins of our friends, just as he pronounced forgiveness long ago. But we cannot tell beforehand who will be saved.

The analogy between the present and the past is further explained by the rest of the New Testament. We know that people are justified by faith in Jesus (Rom. 5:1). Their sins are forgiven, and "there is therefore now no condemnation for those who are in Christ Jesus" (Rom. 8:1). But, to be forgiven, a person must be "in Christ Jesus." At this level, each person must exercise faith:

> Yet we know that a person is not justified by works of the law but through faith in Jesus Christ, so we also *have believed in Christ Jesus*, in order to be justified by *faith in Christ* and not by works of the law, because by works of the law no one will be justified. (Gal. 2:16)

Our faith cannot substitute for another person.

18

Raising Jairus's Daughter
(Matthew 9:18–26)

The kingdom of God reaches out even to the realm of death and to those who seem to be hopeless. We see this reach of the kingdom in the story of the raising of Jairus's daughter:

> While he was saying these things to them, behold, a ruler came in and knelt before him, saying, "My daughter has just died, but come and lay your hand on her, and she will live." And Jesus rose and followed him, with his disciples. And behold, a woman who had suffered from a discharge of blood for twelve years came up behind him and touched the fringe of his garment, for she said to herself, "If I only touch his garment, I will be made well." Jesus turned, and seeing her he said, "Take heart, daughter; your faith has made you well." And instantly the woman was made well. And when Jesus came to the ruler's house and saw the flute players and the crowd making a commotion, he said, "Go away, for the girl is not dead but sleeping." And they laughed at him. But when the crowd had been put outside, he went in and took her by the hand, and the girl arose. And the report of this went through all that district. (Matt. 9:18–26)

This narrative contains two miracles in one. The main story tells about Jesus raising Jairus's daughter from the dead. (Matthew simply identifies Jairus as "a ruler"; Mark 5:22 and Luke 8:41 supply his name.) In the middle we hear about a woman with a flow of blood.

One common element in the two miracles lies in *faith*, which expressed itself in an apparently hopeless situation. The woman had had a flow of blood "for twelve years," which made recovery seem hopeless. Nevertheless, she was confident that she would be healed by touching Jesus's garment. In response, Jesus drew attention to her faith: "Your faith has made you well" (v. 22).

The word *faith* is not used in describing Jairus, but his faith is evident. He expressed confidence even when his daughter was dead (v. 18),[1] making the situation seem hopeless.

Both miracles involved touch. The woman touched Jesus's garment (v. 20). Jesus touched the dead girl by taking her by the hand (v. 25). In both cases, the Mosaic law indicated that the touch communicated uncleanness. A woman with a flow of blood was unclean (Lev. 15:25–27), and a dead body was unclean (Lev. 22:4–6). But instead of Jesus becoming unclean, "cleanness" passed by divine power from him to the unclean person.

The Significance of Healing

The significance of touch is similar to what we saw in the case of healing that we considered in chapter 12. Ceremonial uncleanness symbolizes the deeper, spiritual "uncleanness" of sin. Jesus, by touch, symbolizes his identification with sinners and their sin. This identification foreshadows his substitutionary work of bearing sin on the cross.

Jesus's spiritual healing on the cross reaches the depths of human need. He triumphed over death itself, and this triumph was foreshadowed by his ability to raise Jairus's daughter from the dead.

---

[1] Matthew abbreviates in comparison to the longer descriptions in Mark and Luke. On harmonizing Matthew's account with Mark and Luke, see Vern S. Poythress, *Inerrancy and the Gospels: A God-Centered Approach to the Challenges of Harmonization* (Wheaton, IL: Crossway, 2012), chapter 28.

Jesus said, "the girl is not dead but sleeping" (Matt. 9:24). Were the bystanders mistaken in thinking that she was dead? Luke adds the detail, "her spirit returned" (Luke 8:55), which seems to indicate that she had actually been dead. But in the light of Jesus's power and the kingdom that he was bringing, death itself was redefined as only "sleep," from which Jesus awakens us.[2] The raising of Jairus's daughter clearly foreshadows Jesus's resurrection from the dead. Jesus's resurrection is itself the climactic case of victory when everything seemed hopeless (and the disciples, too, felt hopeless; Luke 24:17, 21).

Just as the woman and Jairus exercised faith in Jesus, we too should exercise faith. Human faith in our time should focus especially on Jesus's resurrection from the dead. Just as Jesus identified by his touch with the uncleanness belonging to the woman and to Jairus's daughter, so he reaches out to identify with the spiritual uncleanness of our sin:

> He himself bore our sins in his body on the tree, that we might die to sin and live to righteousness. By his wounds you have been healed. (1 Pet. 2:24)

Just as Jesus removed uncleanness from the woman and from Jairus's daughter, he removes the guilt of sin from us. Just as he gave new life to the woman and to Jairus's daughter, he gives new spiritual life to us. When we have to face the final "uncleanness" of death itself, he brings us through it by the power of his resurrection:

> I am the resurrection and the life. Whoever believes in me, though he die, yet shall he live, and everyone who lives and believes in me shall never die. Do you believe this? (John 11:25–26)

Clowney's Triangle Applied to Jairus's Daughter

We can summarize the significance of this miracle using Clowney's triangle (fig. 18.1).

---

[2] R. T. France, *The Gospel of Matthew* (Grand Rapids, MI: Eerdmans, 2007), 364.

Fig. 18.1: Clowney's Triangle for Jairus's Daughter

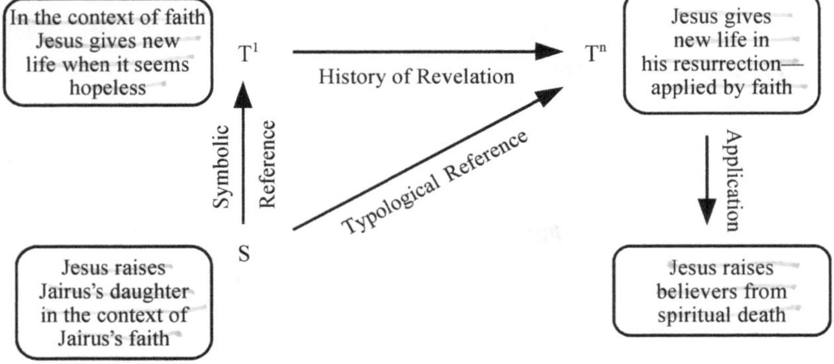

Application for Jairus's Daughter

How does this story apply to us? The story of Jairus's daughter calls for faith in Jesus who can raise the dead, and in particular can raise the sinner who lies in spiritual death.

Healing the Woman with the Flow of Blood

Similar significance belongs to the embedded story, concerning the woman with a flow of blood. The flow of blood was physically debilitating, and in addition rendered the woman ceremonially unclean, which would have led to social exclusion. Ceremonial uncleanness stands for the spiritual uncleanness of sin. Jesus says, "Your faith has made you well" (Matt. 9:22). The verb underlying the English expression "made . . . well" is the Greek word *sōzō*, which is elsewhere used to describe "salvation." The use of this word reinforces the relation between physical healing and spiritual salvation. We can sum up the significance of this healing with a diagram similar to the one for Jairus's daughter (fig. 18.2).

Application for the Story of the Woman with the Flow of Blood

The story applies to us. Through faith we receive healing from sin, in analogy to the woman receiving healing from what made her unclean.

Fig. 18.2: Clowney's Triangle for the Healing
of the Woman with the Flow of Blood

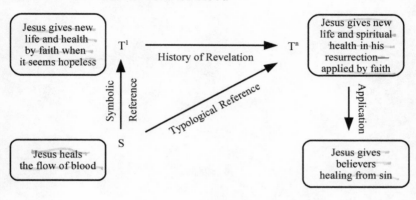

19

Healing Two Blind Men
(Matthew 9:27–31)

The kingdom of God reaches one of the most debilitating diseases, blindness:

> And as Jesus passed on from there, two blind men followed him, crying aloud, "Have mercy on us, Son of David." When he entered the house, the blind men came to him, and Jesus said to them, "Do you believe that I am able to do this?" They said to him, "Yes, Lord." Then he touched their eyes, saying, "According to your faith be it done to you." And their eyes were opened. And Jesus sternly warned them, "See that no one knows about it." But they went away and spread his fame through all that district. (Matt. 9:27–31)

The Significance of Faith

The preceding miracles involving Jairus's daughter and the woman with a flow of blood both emphasized faith (Matt. 9:18, 21–22). If anything, faith is even more prominent in this miracle with the two blind men. Jesus specifically inquired, "Do you *believe* that I am able to do this?" And they answered affirmatively, "Yes, Lord."

Jesus mentioned faith again in the moment of healing, "According to *your faith* be it done to you."

In the Old Testament background, blindness and sight are used symbolically to stand for unbelief and faith:

And he said, "Go, and say to this people:

> "'Keep on hearing, but do not understand;
> keep on *seeing*, but do not *perceive*.'
> Make the heart of this people dull,
>   and their ears heavy,
>   and *blind their eyes*;
> lest they *see* with their eyes,
>   and hear with their ears,
>   and understand with their hearts,
>   and turn and be healed."
>   (Isa. 6:9–10; cf. Matt. 13:14–15)

Matthew picks up this theme, and announces that light has come in the person of Jesus:

> The people dwelling in darkness
>   have seen a great *light*,
> and for those dwelling in the region and shadow of death,
>   on them a *light* has dawned.
>   (Matt. 4:16; quoted from Isa. 9:2)

But have the people seen the light that has dawned on them?

The two blind men had begun to see the light, spiritually speaking. They had faith that Jesus could heal them. In addition, they called him "Son of David" (Matt. 9:27), which hints at their expectation that he was the promised Messiah. Jesus consented to their request and healed their physical blindness. But through the mention of faith, this physical healing is tied to the issue of spiritual healing from spiritual blindness, a healing that moves people from unbelief to faith in Jesus. The relation between physical sight and the spiritual sight of faith is worked out more explicitly in

John 9 (discussed in our chapter 3). But we can see it in this passage as well.

Faith was dawning in the two blind men and in some others who responded to Jesus's earthly miracles and his teaching. But where was this faith headed? It foreshadows the fullness of faith that people have when they believe in the resurrection of Christ and its salvific meaning. "Believe in the Lord Jesus, and you will be saved, you and your household" (Acts 16:31). This full faith issues in praise: "And he rejoiced along with his entire household that he had believed in God" (v. 34).

Clowney's Triangle for Blindness and Faith

We may summarize the significance of this miracle using Clowney's triangle. The faith of the two blind men points to the more mature faith that understands the resurrection of Christ. (See fig. 19.1.)

Fig. 19.1: Clowney's Triangle for the Two Believing Blind Men

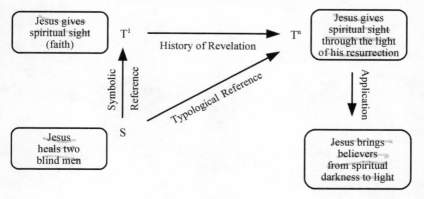

Application

How does this passage apply to us? The main application is a natural extension of the meaning of faith in Christ's resurrection. Throughout the gospel age, God calls people to turn from darkness to light by faith in Christ, and this gospel comes also to the Gentiles:

. . . delivering you from your people and from the Gentiles— to whom I am sending you to *open their eyes*, so that they may turn from darkness to *light* and from the power of Satan to God, that they may receive forgiveness of sins and a place among those who are sanctified by faith in me. (Acts 26:17–18)

20

Healing a Mute Demoniac
(Matthew 9:32–34)

Continuing the point made in the story of the Gadarene demoniacs
(Matt. 8:28–34), Matthew provides another case of Jesus's power
to heal demonized people:

> As they were going away, behold, a demon-oppressed man
> who was mute was brought to him. And when the demon had
> been cast out, the mute man spoke. And the crowds marveled,
> saying, "Never was anything like this seen in Israel." But the
> Pharisees said, "He casts out demons by the prince of demons."
> (Matt. 9:32–34)

Significance of Healing the Mute Man

In substance, this story is similar to the one about the Gadarene
demoniacs. But it adds a note about the opposition from the Pharisees; they charged that Jesus "casts out demons by the prince of
demons" (v. 34). The Pharisees were expressing opposition not only
to this particular act of deliverance but to all the cases where Jesus
cast out demons. They said, "He casts out *demons*," with the word
demons in the plural. The Pharisees, of course, were wrong in their

evaluation. But the fact that their evaluation was a general evaluation raises the question of why Jesus cast out demons on so many occasions. The answer is fairly obvious: Satan's power is overcome. If so, the whole collection of instances of deliverance from demons points forward to the decisive and climactic deliverance from the power of Satan and death in the crucifixion and the resurrection.

We refer back to chapter 16 for a more extended discussion of casting out demons. We will again discuss the opposition between the kingdom of God and the kingdom of Satan when we come to chapter 24.

21

Many Healings
(Matthew 9:35–38)

The scope of Jesus's healing ministry is further reinforced by the imagery of a plentiful harvest:

> And Jesus went throughout all the cities and villages, teaching in their synagogues and proclaiming the gospel of the kingdom and healing every disease and every affliction. When he saw the crowds, he had compassion for them, because they were harassed and helpless, like sheep without a shepherd. Then he said to his disciples, "The harvest is plentiful, but the laborers are few; therefore pray earnestly to the Lord of the harvest to send out laborers into his harvest." (Matt. 9:35–38)

Like the earlier summary of many healings (chapter 11; Matt. 4:23–25), this summary serves to remind us that Matthew is giving us a few key miracles among many that characterized Jesus's public ministry and the gospel of the kingdom of God. In fact, Matthew 9:35 is almost identical to Matthew 4:23 (see the parallel-column comparison on the following page)

Both verses mention Christ's teaching and "proclaiming the gospel of the kingdom." His teaching is teaching about the good news of the kingdom of God. The healings manifest the power of God's kingdom, coming to deliver people. The reality of deliverance from "every disease and every affliction" is good news. As we saw in chapter 11, in looking at Matthew 4:23–25, this description also implies that physical healing is part of the larger complex of events in which God is coming and acting in power in fulfillment of the Old Testament prophecies of salvation. Salvation, comprehensively viewed, includes more than healing diseases. At its heart, it is healing from sin. And so the miracles are signs of the kingdom.

Comparison of Summary Passages about Healing

Matthew 4:23	Matthew 9:35
And he went throughout all Galilee, teaching in their synagogues and proclaiming the gospel of the kingdom and healing every disease and every affliction among the people.	And Jesus went throughout all the cities and villages, teaching in their synagogues and proclaiming the gospel of the kingdom and healing every disease and every affliction.

Each of the two summary passages, Matthew 4:23–25 and 9:35–38, lies at the end of a larger section of narrative in Matthew, and serves as a transition to a block of teaching. Matthew 4:23–25 introduces the teaching on the kingdom of God in Matthew 5–7, while Matthew 9:35–38 introduces Jesus's instruction of his disciples in Matthew 10.

The Significance of Healings

Matthew 9:36–38 includes two further elements that were not explicit in the earlier summary in 4:23–25. Verse 36 has the imagery of shepherd and sheep. The people were "like sheep without a shepherd," and Jesus had "compassion for them." Jesus himself was functioning like a shepherd to them. The imagery reflects Ezekiel 34, where Israel has false shepherds who are not real shepherds at all, and where God promises to be the true shepherd. He will do so through "one shepherd, my servant David" (Ezek. 34:23), that is, through the Messiah, the son of David. Matthew does not explicitly comment on the significance of Ezekiel 34, but the use of shepherding imagery evokes it as a background.

The prophecy in Ezekiel 34 describes comprehensive salvation, and so its scope includes more than just physical healing. The hard-hearted, disobedient Israelites of Ezekiel's time needed a renewal of heart (Ezek. 36:25–28), not merely a renewal of body. This renewal comes through God himself and his Messiah. By linking Jesus's healing ministry with "the gospel of the kingdom," Matthew indicates that Jesus is the Messiah, the agent of comprehensive salvation and renewal. And so the summary in Matthew 9:35–38 points to Jesus's climactic work in the crucifixion and resurrection. Jesus's death and resurrection takes place on behalf of his people, so that they too will experience new life through him (Ezekiel 37; Matt. 28:19–20).

Matthew 9:37–38 introduces a second image, the image of a harvest. The spring and autumn harvest feasts in Israel, namely the feast of weeks and the feast of tabernacles, both function as types or shadows, pointing forward to the final harvest that consists in definitive salvation. This harvest takes place through the gathering of peoples as well as the blessing of superlative abundance from God:

> On this mountain the LORD of hosts will make for *all peoples*
>   *a feast* of rich food, a feast of well-aged wine,
>   of rich food full of marrow, of aged wine well refined.
> And he will swallow up on this mountain
>   the covering that is cast over all peoples,
>   the veil that is spread over all nations.
> He will swallow up death forever;
> and the Lord GOD will wipe away tears from all faces,
>   and the reproach of his people he will take away from all
>   the earth,
>   for the LORD has spoken.
> It will be said on that day,
>   "Behold, this is our God; we have waited for him, that he
>   might save us.

> This is the LORD; we have waited for him;
> let us be glad and rejoice in his salvation." (Isa. 25:6–9)

The final gathering of peoples takes place at the second coming (Matt. 24:31). The feast is the feast of the kingdom of God, which Jesus proclaimed in the parable of the wedding feast (22:1–14) and the parable of the ten virgins (25:10). He further hinted at it when he mentioned reclining "at table with Abraham, Isaac, and Jacob in the kingdom of heaven" (8:11). Gentiles are included. Jesus acted out the feast, by way of foreshadowing, in his fellowship with tax collectors and sinners (9:10–13).

Though the final harvest comes at the second coming, harvesting also took place in an initial way as soon as the kingdom of God was inaugurated in Jesus's earthly ministry. The harvest expands at the day of Pentecost. People are "harvested" when God brings them into his kingdom and into fellowship with Christ. In Matthew 9:37–38 the harvest calls for laborers. This call for laborers prepares us for Jesus's instructions in Matthew 10:1–11:1, where he appointed and guided his disciples as laborers. He sent them "to the lost sheep of the house of Israel" (10:6), recapitulating the imagery of sheep. The labor of the disciples reaches a new phase of fulfillment in the Great Commission of Matthew 28:18–20. In the Great Commission, the disciples go not only to Israel but now to "all nations" (v. 19). They do so on the basis of the victory that Jesus has already achieved: "All authority in heaven and on earth has been given to me" (v. 18). The harvest will reach its fullness when Christ returns.

Clowney's Triangle for Shepherding and Harvesting

We may summarize both the imagery of shepherding and the imagery of harvest laborers using Clowney's triangle (fig. 21.1).

Application to People as Sheep and as Harvest

The application of these verses to this age of gospel proclamation is natural. People in all nations form the target for present-day ministry. The gospel invites people from every nation to come to Jesus, who is the divine shepherd. The people who receive the gospel are sheep who need shepherding. Jesus's compassion reaches out to them. And the same people are a harvest, whom Jesus is gathering through the laborers that he commissions and empowers.

Fig. 21.1: Clowney's Triangle for Shepherding and Harvesting

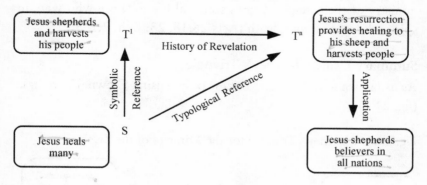

Commissioning the Twelve to Work Miracles

In connection with Jesus's work of healing we find shortly afterward a description of powerful works for which he commissioned the Twelve:

> And proclaim as you go, saying, "The kingdom of heaven is at hand." Heal the sick, raise the dead, cleanse lepers, cast out demons. (Matt. 10:7–8)

The twelve disciples were here empowered to work miracles that imitate Jesus's miracles of healing and exorcism. These miracles accompanied the proclamation, "The kingdom of heaven is at hand." The miracles were signs of the kingdom, signs of God's mighty saving power at work. The disciples worked miracles not because of any power innate in them but by the power of Jesus's commission. Earlier, Jesus healed the centurion's servant at a distance (Matt. 8:13). It was enough for Jesus to speak the word, because his word had the power of the kingdom within it. Likewise, Jesus's word of commission guaranteed the power by which the disciples worked miracles.

As with all the healing miracles, these miracles through the twelve disciples point forward to the supreme miracle of Jesus's resurrection. Jesus's resurrection is the foundation on the basis of which the gospel then goes out and people from all nations become disciples (Matt. 28:19). After Jesus's resurrection, his disciples carry the message of the kingdom of God in a new phase of activity. The ministry of the disciples brings spiritual life to those who were in spiritual darkness and death (Acts 26:18, 23; Eph. 2:1–3).

Summary Using Clowney's Triangle

As usual, we may summarize these points using Clowney's triangle (fig. 21.2).

Fig. 21.2: Clowney's Triangle for the Miracles of the Twelve

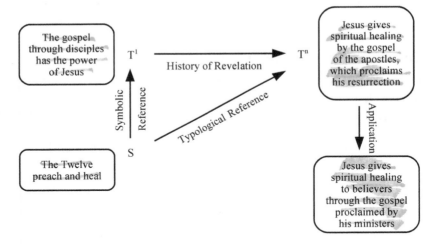

Application

The passage has an application to us. Jesus still commissions ministers in his name, who proclaim the gospel of the apostles. And Jesus still heals people today from the misery of sin. Jesus's ministry today still leads to the response of praising him and glorifying his name.

22

Healing a Withered Hand
(Matthew 12:9–14)

The section of Matthew comprising chapters 11–13 focuses more than previous sections on the issue of wisdom and discernment. Who will discern the meaning of the parables in Matthew 13? And who will recognize the signs of the kingdom in Matthew 11–12? In this context we meet the narrative of the man with a withered hand:

> He went on from there and entered their synagogue. And a man was there with a withered hand. And they asked him, "Is it lawful to heal on the Sabbath?"—so that they might accuse him. He said to them, "Which one of you who has a sheep, if it falls into a pit on the Sabbath, will not take hold of it and lift it out? Of how much more value is a man than a sheep! So it is lawful to do good on the Sabbath." Then he said to the man, "Stretch out your hand." And the man stretched it out, and it was restored, healthy like the other. But the Pharisees went out and conspired against him, how to destroy him. (Matt. 12:9–14)

The Significance of Healing

This episode of healing is paired with the preceding episode containing a controversy about keeping the Sabbath (Matt. 12:1–8).

At the end of this preceding episode, Jesus makes a key statement: "For the Son of Man is lord of the Sabbath" (v. 8). The healing of the man with a withered hand raises the same issue, because it took place on the Sabbath: "Is it lawful to heal on the Sabbath?" (v. 10). Jesus replied with a yes answer, both in his words and in his deeds. He argued the case by comparison with a sheep fallen into a pit (v. 11). By implication, the man with a withered hand is more valuable than a sheep, because he is a sheep of the house of Israel.

Because of the linkage with the preceding episode, Jesus's healing does not justify itself purely by a general argument that "it is lawful to do good on the Sabbath" (v. 12); it is supremely appropriate to do good when the actor is "the Son of Man," who "is lord of the Sabbath" (v. 8).

The Sabbath in Israel has its origin in creation: God created the world in six days and rested on the seventh (Ex. 20:11). It also has a connection with redemption. The people are to give rest to their workers because God rescued them from slavery in Egypt (Deut. 5:14–15). Jesus is the Son of Man, who is Redeemer of Israel and Redeemer of the world. The key background for the expression "the Son of Man" lies in Daniel 7:13. Daniel 7:13 depicts a human figure, who supersedes the bestial kingdoms of this world. Symbolically, it represents man triumphing over beast, against the background of the dominion given to Adam in Genesis 1:28. This passage is therefore an Old Testament background for the concept of Christ as the last Adam in 1 Corinthians 15:45. He is the representative head of the new order of humanity, who will bring new creation to consummation. The Sabbath as a sign of final rest points to him. So it is eminently suitable that he should accomplish works of healing *especially* on the Sabbath.

The final Sabbath rest began for Christ personally when he finished his work on earth and was raised to new life on the third day. Since Christ's people are in union with him, they have already entered the new life of healing in him. But they also await the consummation at his second coming (Heb. 4:9–10).

Clowney's Triangle for Sabbath Healing

We may summarize the significance of this Sabbath healing using Clowney's triangle (fig. 22.1).

Fig. 22.1: Clowney's Triangle for the Sabbath Healing of the Man with the Withered Hand

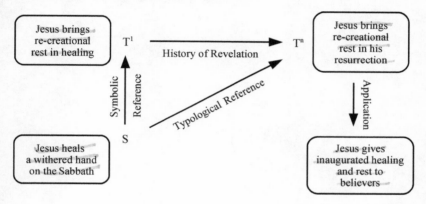

Application of the Story

We have touched on application already by reflecting on how God's people enter inaugurated rest through union with Christ's resurrection achievement. This episode encourages readers to rejoice in the inauguration of new creation in Christ, and to wait expectantly for his return and the consummation of the new creation.

23

Many Healings
(Matthew 12:15–21)

Matthew 12:15–21 contains another summary statement about the many healings that Jesus was performing:

> Jesus, aware of this, withdrew from there. And many followed him, and he healed them all and ordered them not to make him known. This was to fulfill what was spoken by the prophet Isaiah:
>
> "Behold, my servant whom I have chosen,
>   my beloved with whom my soul is well pleased.
> I will put my Spirit upon him,
>   and he will proclaim justice to the Gentiles.
> He will not quarrel or cry aloud,
>   nor will anyone hear his voice in the streets;
> a bruised reed he will not break,
>   and a smoldering wick he will not quench,
> until he brings justice to victory;
>   and in his name the Gentiles will hope."

The Significance of Healings

This summary does not simply repeat previous summaries of Jesus's healing ministry. It probes the significance of the healings by quoting from one of the servant passages in Isaiah (42:1–4). In our earlier discussion in chapter 11 of the summary statement in Matthew 4:23–25, we already looked at Matthew 8:16–17 as well. It quotes from Isaiah 53 and thereby connects Jesus's ministry with the servant passages in Isaiah. Isaiah 53 prophesies Christ's suffering and death. Isaiah 42:1–4 has a complementary focus. It speaks about justice and mercy coming to the weak and fainting. Christ's healing ministry shows the compassion that fulfills Isaiah 42:1–4. It confirms his messianic role. At the same time, the connection of Christ's work with Isaiah 42:1–4 indicates that healing is part of a larger program of kingdom deliverance that includes the achievement of justice, not only for Israel but for all nations (Isa. 42:1, 4, 6). As part of Christ's role in bringing justice to the nations, later verses in Isaiah 42 indicate that he will

> . . . open the eyes that are blind,
>   to bring out the prisoners from the dungeon,
>   from the prison those who sit in darkness. (42:7)

Christ's resurrection opens blind eyes to faith and rescues people from the prison of sin. His resurrection is the foundation for the full achievement of both justice and compassion throughout the world. Application today comes as Christ gives spiritual sight and deliverance. He rules in justice over those who belong to him. Those who are delivered begin to join in praising him for his grace.

Clowney's Triangle for Justice and Compassion

We may use Clowney's triangle to summarize the significance of the themes of justice and compassion in Jesus's healing ministry (fig. 23.1).

Fig. 23.1: Clowney's Triangle for Justice and Compassionate Healing

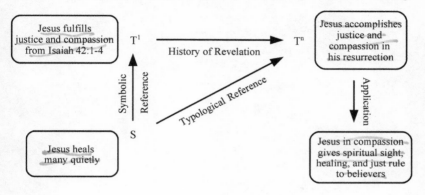

24

A Blind and Mute Man
(Matthew 12:22–23)

Matthew next provides an account of Jesus healing a demonized blind and mute man:

> Then a demon-oppressed man who was blind and mute was brought to him, and he healed him, so that the man spoke and saw. And all the people were amazed, and said, "Can this be the Son of David?" (Matt. 12:22–23)

This account is similar to an earlier one where Jesus healed a demonized mute man (Matt. 9:32–34). Both of these accounts, together with the episode about the Gadarene demoniacs (Matt. 8:28–34), contain the theme of Christ delivering people from the demonic realm.

What distinct emphasis, if any, do we see in this latest account, in Matthew 12:22–23? Accompanying this latest narrative is a fuller account of the opposition from the Pharisees:

> But when the Pharisees heard it, they said, "It is only by Beelzebul, the prince of demons, that this man casts out demons." Knowing their thoughts, he said to them, "Every kingdom

divided against itself is laid waste, and no city or house divided against itself will stand. And if Satan casts out Satan, he is divided against himself. How then will his kingdom stand? And if I cast out demons by Beelzebul, by whom do your sons cast them out? Therefore they will be your judges. But if it is by the Spirit of God that I cast out demons, then the kingdom of God has come upon you. Or how can someone enter a strong man's house and plunder his goods, unless he first binds the strong man? Then indeed he may plunder his house. Whoever is not with me is against me, and whoever does not gather with me scatters. Therefore I tell you, every sin and blasphemy will be forgiven people, but the blasphemy against the Spirit will not be forgiven. And whoever speaks a word against the Son of Man will be forgiven, but whoever speaks against the Holy Spirit will not be forgiven, either in this age or in the age to come.

"Either make the tree good and its fruit good, or make the tree bad and its fruit bad, for the tree is known by its fruit. You brood of vipers! How can you speak good, when you are evil? For out of the abundance of the heart the mouth speaks. The good person out of his good treasure brings forth good, and the evil person out of his evil treasure brings forth evil. I tell you, on the day of judgment people will give account for every careless word they speak, for by your words you will be justified, and by your words you will be condemned." (Matt. 12:24–37)

The polarity between the two kingdoms, the kingdom of God and the kingdom of Satan, is vividly underscored. In this context, Jesus warns the Pharisees that their very words condemn them. They are themselves on the wrong side of the conflict.

The polarity between the two kingdoms has its roots in the realm of invisible spiritual powers, with God on one side and the demons on the other. But the opposition from the Pharisees indicates that the conflict extends into the human realm as well. A human being can be oppressed by demons, with the result that he can neither see nor speak. But human beings can also position themselves by their own thinking in opposition to God and his kingdom, even to the point of blaspheming the Holy Spirit (v. 32). The deepest opposition to God is found not merely in physical debility but in debility of the heart, which issues in debility in one's words.

In fact, "debility" is too weak a word. People are not merely weak or sick; they are rebels against God. They are spiritually dead (Eph. 2:1, 5). Physical blindness, as we have pointed out, can symbolize spiritual blindness. The demonized man was physically blind and mute. The Pharisees were not demonized in the same way, but they showed themselves to be spiritually blind. And they were mute with respect to expressing the truths of the kingdom of God. They were worse than mute; they spoke *against* God and his kingdom.

The climactic fight of the two kingdoms is found in the crucifixion and the resurrection. Satan energized Judas the betrayer and those who plotted to arrest and kill Jesus (Matt. 26:3–4, 14–16). Unlike Luke 22:3, 22:53, and John 13:27, Matthew does not explicitly mention Satan's presence during the trial and crucifixion. But we can infer the presence of a demonic background from the polarity of the two kingdoms in Matthew 12:24–37. Jesus achieved in his crucifixion and resurrection the decisive triumph over Satan. As the representative for his people, he delivered them once and for all from the kingdom of Satan. He "plunders the strong man" (see Matt. 12:29) by his resurrection even more thoroughly than he did by his exorcisms during his earthly ministry.

Jesus's victory over Satan underscores the greatness of God's power. The kingdom of God and the kingdom of Satan are not equally matched kingdoms. Satan is not a second "god" comparable to the true God. Satan is powerful, but he is only a creature. His rebellion against God cannot succeed. The demons are subject to Christ's authority. Satan and his evil agents brought about the crucifixion of Christ. But God's hand directed the entire process, and he brought about salvation through the very events that Satan intended for evil:

> this Jesus, delivered up according to the definite plan and foreknowledge of God, you crucified and killed by the hands of

lawless men. God raised him up, loosing the pangs of death, because it was not possible for him to be held by it. (Acts 2:23–24)

Clowney's Triangle Applied to the Two Kingdoms

As usual, we can summarize the significance of the healing of the demonized man using Clowney's triangle (fig. 24.1).

Fig. 24.1: Clowney's Triangle for Christ's Triumph over Satan

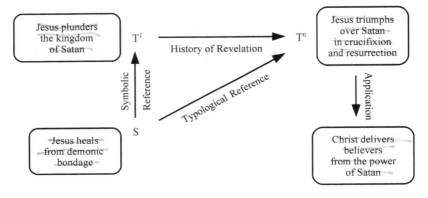

Application

The work of Christ is applied to us when we are delivered from bondage to the worldly kingdom of darkness, over which Satan rules (1 John 5:19):

> He has delivered us from the domain of darkness and transferred us to the kingdom of his beloved Son, in whom we have redemption, the forgiveness of sins. (Col. 1:13–14)

We should celebrate his deliverance with praise, and rejoice that Satan is a defeated foe.

25

Feeding the 5,000
(Matthew 14:13–21)

The section of Matthew comprising chapters 14 through 18 has some enhanced focus on the care for God's people within the kingdom of God. It is fitting that, within this section, we find two miracles in which Jesus provided care in the form of physical food. In the first of the two episodes of miraculous multiplication of food, he fed 5,000 men (plus women and children):

> Now when Jesus heard this, he withdrew from there in a boat to a desolate place by himself. But when the crowds heard it, they followed him on foot from the towns. When he went ashore he saw a great crowd, and he had compassion on them and healed their sick. Now when it was evening, the disciples came to him and said, "This is a desolate place, and the day is now over; send the crowds away to go into the villages and buy food for themselves." But Jesus said, "They need not go away; you give them something to eat." They said to him, "We have only five loaves here and two fish." And he said, "Bring them here to me." Then he ordered the crowds to sit down on the grass, and taking the five loaves and the two fish, he looked up to heaven and said a blessing. Then he broke the loaves and

gave them to the disciples, and the disciples gave them to the crowds. And they all ate and were satisfied. And they took up twelve baskets full of the broken pieces left over. And those who ate were about five thousand men, besides women and children. (Matt. 14:13–21)

The Significance of Feeding the 5,000

In this first account (the second is the feeding of the 4,000; 15:32–39), we get a clue about the significance of the miracle from Jesus's attitude: "he had compassion on them and healed their sick" (14:14). The mention of compassion and healing recalls Matthew 9:35–36 (see chapter 21). Providing food is one way in which Jesus acted as a shepherd to provide for the needs of the sheep of Israel. The background in Ezekiel 34 also gives attention to the imagery of food for the sheep:

> And I will *feed them* on the mountains of Israel, by the ravines, and in all the inhabited places of the country. I will *feed them with good pasture*, and on the mountain heights of Israel shall be their *grazing land*. There they shall lie down in *good grazing land*, and on *rich pasture* they shall *feed* on the mountains of Israel. . . . I will *feed them* in justice. (Ezek. 34:13–14, 16)

In the background to Matthew's account there also lies the miracle in which Elisha fed a hundred men (2 Kings 4:42–44). And then we think of God feeding Israel the manna in the wilderness. The account in John 6 made the connection with the manna more explicit (as we saw in chapter 3). But it is there in Matthew as well, since the general theme of God's provision for his people links all the passages.

The climactic provision of spiritual food took place with Jesus's crucifixion and resurrection, which functioned as the new Passover with Jesus as the Passover Lamb (Matt. 26:26–29). This provision through Christ will be consummated in the feast of the new heaven and the new earth (Rev. 19:9).

Clowney's Triangle for Feeding the 5,000

Our earlier reflections on John 6 have shown how Clowney's triangle applies. It should be clear that the same diagram also holds for Matthew's account, even though Matthew has not been as explicit about the fact that Jesus is the bread from heaven. Instead, the implicit connections in Matthew lead to a greater prominence for the fact that Jesus is the messianic shepherd over Israel. Accordingly, fig. 25.1 shows Clowney's triangle, slightly revised from John 6 (see fig. 3.1) in order to emphasize Jesus's role as shepherd and Jesus as Passover Lamb.

Fig. 25.1: Clowney's Triangle for Feeding the 5,000, in Matthew

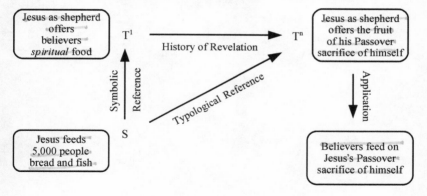

Application

Jesus accomplished salvation through fulfilling the Passover. He was the final Passover sacrifice. This sacrifice provides spiritual food for us. The miracle of feeding 5,000 invites us to receive the benefit of his sacrifice, as we feed on him.

26

Walking on Water
(Matthew 14:22–33)

Matthew describes a powerful miracle in which Jesus walked on water and Peter began to do so as well:

> Immediately he made the disciples get into the boat and go before him to the other side, while he dismissed the crowds. And after he had dismissed the crowds, he went up on the mountain by himself to pray. When evening came, he was there alone, but the boat by this time was a long way from the land, beaten by the waves, for the wind was against them. And in the fourth watch of the night he came to them, walking on the sea. But when the disciples saw him walking on the sea, they were terrified, and said, "It is a ghost!" and they cried out in fear. But immediately Jesus spoke to them, saying, "Take heart; it is I. Do not be afraid."
>
> And Peter answered him, "Lord, if it is you, command me to come to you on the water." He said, "Come." So Peter got out of the boat and walked on the water and came to Jesus. But when he saw the wind, he was afraid, and beginning to sink he cried out, "Lord, save me." Jesus immediately reached out his hand and took hold of him, saying to him, "O you of little

faith, why did you doubt?" And when they got into the boat, the wind ceased. And those in the boat worshiped him, saying, "Truly you are the Son of God." (Matt. 14:22–33)

This encounter between Jesus and his disciples included several kinds of threats that Jesus overcame. First, the passage calls to mind an earlier storm, where the disciples feared for their lives (Matt. 8:23–27; see chapter 15). Does Matthew 14:22–33 describe a similar storm? In Matthew 14, we do not hear of a violent storm, but still the disciples were in difficulty because of the waves: "the boat by this time was a long way from the land, *beaten by the waves*, for *the wind was against them*" (Matt. 14:24). By the conclusion of the story, the wind has ceased (v. 32). So relief has come for this first difficulty of theirs.

Second, the disciples were terrified when they saw a figure walking on the sea. They thought it was a ghost (v. 26). Jesus responded to their fear by identifying himself and telling them to "Take heart" (v. 27). The passage does not report explicitly the disciples' reaction to Jesus's words. But Peter, as a kind of representative disciple, was obviously relieved and even emboldened. So it is easy to conclude that Jesus's words overcame the terror that the disciples had experienced.

A third difficulty arose because of Peter's boldness. Peter began to walk on the water, but then sank. "But when he saw the wind, he was afraid, and beginning to sink he cried out, 'Lord, save me'" (v. 30). Jesus reached out his hand and saved him. So the third difficulty was overcome.

The Significance of the Miracle

So what is the significance of this cluster of miracles? Taking the three difficulties together, we can surely say that the miracle indicates Jesus's power and willingness to overcome all kinds of difficulty. But that is a very general summary. As we attend to the details of this particular story, can we see a more specific focus?

One theme that comes into focus is the theme of fear and faith. The disciples began with fear. Peter showed a kind of faith in his proposal to come to Jesus. But his faith failed him. He began to sink, but at least he had faith enough to call out to Jesus to save him. Jesus in response explicitly brought up the theme of faith: "O you of *little faith*, why did you *doubt*?" (v. 31). The story ends with a confession that shows something about the disciples' faith: "And those in the boat worshiped him, saying, 'Truly you are the Son of God'" (v. 33).

Within the narrative, Peter plays a striking role. It is dramatic enough that Jesus was walking on the water. But Peter also? And what motivated Peter to propose to Jesus that he should come to him on the water? Elsewhere in the Gospels Peter has boldness at times. And boldness can mean overconfidence, as when Peter promised, "I will never fall away" (Matt. 26:33), and, "Even if I must die with you, I will not deny you!" (26:35). Was his boldness this time due to mere bravado? Was it contaminated with pride, saying in effect, "I'll show what I can do"? Or was it genuine faith? The story as recorded in Matthew does not give us a complete inward analysis of Peter. It says that when Peter "saw the wind, he was afraid" (Matt. 14:30). And Jesus did say that Peter had "little faith." Beyond that, we find ourselves making guesses about the complexity of Peter's heart.

Peter is a mixed figure in this story. He had faith, but it was "little faith," and subject to doubt and fear. Part of the point of the story is that Jesus was gracious in dealing with such disciples. And Jesus encouraged growth in faith.

Jesus as the Son of God

Faith here was not faith in faith, but faith in Jesus. At the conclusion of the story, the disciples confessed, "Truly you are the Son of God" (Matt. 14:33). Faith in Jesus needs to be generated by who Jesus is. And who is he? "The Son of God." That title recurs in Matthew. In Matthew 16, Peter's key confession says, "You are the Christ, the Son of the living God" (16:16). At Jesus's baptism the voice from heaven said, "This is my beloved Son, with whom I am well pleased" (3:17). The Old Testament background includes the language of "son" used for the Davidic king whom God enthrones on Mount Zion (Ps. 2:6–7). God set David on the throne of Israel. But David points forward to a greater descendant of David, the messianic son (Isa. 9:6–7). And this son will be God as well as man. The language of the Great Commission in Matthew 28:19 presupposes the deity of the Son by putting him together in name and in honor with the Father and the Spirit.

Matthew 14:22–33 does not make everything quite as explicit as what we receive by reading the whole of Matthew. But the reality of Jesus's divine Sonship is already there. Jesus exercised divine power by walking on the water. In the background are Old Testament passages where God calmed the sea (Ps. 107:29) and where God trampled on the waters:

> . . . who alone stretched out the heavens
> and *trampled* the waves of the sea. (Job 9:8)

> You *trampled* the sea with your horses,
> the surging of mighty waters. (Hab. 3:15)

The sea in its tumult is a symbol for what is unmasterable; only God can master it.

In the light of this symbolism, we can see a deeper significance in Jesus's self-identification. He said, "It is I" (Matt. 14:27). The underlying Greek expression (*ego eimi*) can indeed mean "It is I." And that is the proper translation in the context, given that the disciples thought they were seeing a ghost. We expect an appropriate response in which Jesus would give a personal identification to his disciples. But in addition, the expression in verse 27 is the same in Greek as the famous expression in John 8:58, where Jesus said, "Before Abraham was, *I am*." In John 8:58 the Jews saw Jesus's statement as blasphemous, not only because he appeared to be claiming to be eternal, but because the expression "I am" reflects the special name of God that God reveals to Moses in Exodus 3:14:

> God said to Moses, "I AM WHO I AM." And he said, "Say this to the people of Israel, 'I AM has sent me to you.'"

So is there an allusion to Exodus 3:14 in Matthew 14:27? The passage in Matthew does not become explicit about this allusion in the same way that John 8:58 does. Nevertheless, the appearance of a figure walking on water provides a context in which it is natural to think of a *divine* figure with power over the sea. So the association with the name "I am" is natural. That association forms an additional layer beyond the obvious layer in which Jesus indicates to the disciples his identity—"It is I." The two layers are a coherent unity, since the power of Jesus to walk on water raises the question of identity in a powerful way. The response indicates that the figure that the disciples saw was not a ghost but the master with whom they were already familiar. At the same time, that sense of "familiarity" was challenged by what Jesus revealed about himself. He is "the Son of God," and the disciples were only beginning to grasp all that that implies.

How does this miracle connect forward to the crucifixion and the resurrection? The miracle has at least two prongs, as we have seen. One prong concerns the identity of Jesus as the Son of God. This revelation of Jesus's identity points forward to the *fuller* revelation of his identity that took place in the cross and the resurrection. These climactic events reveal that he is the divine and human mediator of salvation to the world. Fittingly, the centurion (a Gentile) confessed at the cross, "Truly this was the Son of God" (Matt. 27:54). And after the resurrection, in giving the Great Commission, Jesus identified himself as "the Son" (Matt. 28:19).

The second prong of this miracle concerns the exercise of faith. Peter had faith, but it was "little faith." The challenge to have faith reaches its climax with the cross and resurrection. At this climactic point the challenge becomes, "Have faith in Jesus and in what he has accomplished in the crucifixion and the resurrection."

The picture of Jesus holding out his hand and rescuing Peter represents the climax of the story in Matthew 14:22–33. Jesus as the Savior of the world now holds out his hand, so to speak, to rescue us from sin and death. Peter was sinking down into the waters of death. He could have drowned. So what happened to Peter is a suitable symbol for Jesus's work as Savior from sin and death.

Summary in Clowney's Triangle

As usual, we can summarize the significance of the miracle using Clowney's triangle (fig. 26.1).

Fig. 26.1: Clowney's Triangle for Walking on Water

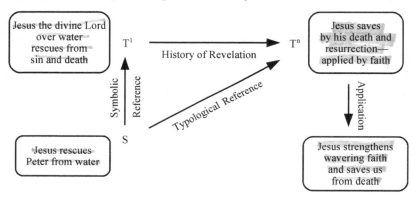

Application to Us

Application of this miracle to us in the gospel age depends on two prongs of continuity: (1) Jesus is the same divine Lord who has power over the sea and over death. (2) People have wavering faith, which mixes faith and unbelief. Their wavering faith is analogous to what happened with Peter. Jesus lives in heaven, victorious over death. By the Holy Spirit he reaches out his hand into people's lives, as they cry out, "Lord, save me."[1] He pulls them out of the sea of sin and death. We praise him that in his mercy he is willing to strengthen our wavering faith. And he is able to rescue us absolutely, because his power rules over everything.

---

[1] As a Calvinist, I believe that a sinner's cry to Christ for salvation is always empowered by a preceding work of the Holy Spirit in the sinner's heart. We are saved by the sovereign grace of God. In Peter's case, the sovereignty of God in salvation is exemplified in Jesus's statement, "You did not choose me, but I chose you" (John 15:16). Matthew 14:30 gives us a picture of one event in the middle of a complex process involving the continuing work of the Holy Spirit in Peter's life.

27

Healing Many
(Matthew 14:34–36)

Matthew 14:34–36 provides another summary statement about Jesus healing many people:

> And when they had crossed over, they came to land at Gennesaret. And when the men of that place recognized him, they sent around to all that region and brought to him all who were sick and implored him that they might only touch the fringe of his garment. And as many as touched it were made well.

Like the earlier summaries in Matthew 4:23–25 (chapter 11), Matthew 9:35–38 (chapter 21), and Matthew 12:15–21 (chapter 23), this summary reminds us that the miracles that Matthew specifically records belong to a larger story of the coming of the kingdom of God in the work of Jesus. Jesus did many more miracles besides those recorded. And all these miracles show the saving, healing power of God at work. The summaries invite us to see each particular miracle as part of the broad plan of God to bring salvation.

Matthew 14:34–36, like 4:23–25, mentions that people were active in bringing others who were sick. Matthew 14:34–36 devotes more attention to this aspect than does any one of the preceding summaries. Men brought the sick (v. 35), as in Matthew 4:24. But in addition, "they sent around to all that region" (14:35). They engaged in a fairly elaborate process of conveying around the region the news of Jesus's presence. They also made urgent requests to Jesus: they "implored him that they might only touch the fringe of his garment" (v. 36). These activities reveal a more general principle: the kingdom of God grows through the activities of networks of people in communities, as well as through the activities of individuals. The initial "network" is Jesus himself, to whom people come and with whom they are united by faith through the Holy Spirit.

How does this principle manifest itself in the climactic events of Jesus's crucifixion and resurrection? Jesus's accomplishment brings salvation that transforms individuals and networks and communities. The consummation of his salvation comes in the new Jerusalem (Rev. 21:2, 10), which is both a community and individuals. Within the gospel age, the church is a community composed of individuals. Concerned people can serve in spreading the news of Jesus and bringing others to find salvation through him.

Summary Using Clowney's Triangle

We may summarize the significance of this communal dimension using Clowney's triangle (fig. 27.1).

Application

As an application, we should reckon with how God uses the church as a community in bringing salvation to his people. He works both in individuals and in the church as the body of Christ. We should praise him for his wisdom in the way in which he works.

Fig. 27.1: Clowney's Triangle for the Communal
Dimension of the Church

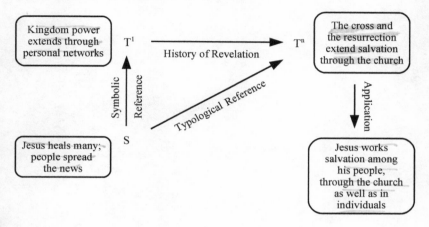

28

The Syrophoenician Woman
(Matthew 15:21–28)

Matthew's next miracle report involves a Canaanite woman from Tyre and Sidon:

> And Jesus went away from there and withdrew to the district of Tyre and Sidon. And behold, a Canaanite woman from that region came out and was crying, "Have mercy on me, O Lord, Son of David; my daughter is severely oppressed by a demon." But he did not answer her a word. And his disciples came and begged him, saying, "Send her away, for she is crying out after us." He answered, "I was sent only to the lost sheep of the house of Israel." But she came and knelt before him, saying, "Lord, help me." And he answered, "It is not right to take the children's bread and throw it to the dogs." She said, "Yes, Lord, yet even the dogs eat the crumbs that fall from their masters' table." Then Jesus answered her, "O woman, great is your faith! Be it done for you as you desire." And her daughter was healed instantly. (Matt. 15:21–28)

Like the story of the centurion in Matthew 8:5–13, this miracle concerns a Gentile. More than that, this Gentile was a "Canaanite"

(Matt. 15:22), which means that she was associated with the people groups whom Joshua long ago was commissioned to destroy (Deut. 7:2; Josh 6:17, 21). Superficially, one might reason that she was beyond the scope of God's mercy. Moreover, Jesus at first did not respond to her. When he did respond, it was with a pointed reference to his duty as a shepherd toward the "lost sheep of the house of Israel." In the Gospel of Matthew as a whole, the time would come when Jesus sends the disciples out to "all nations" (Matt. 28:19). But that time had not yet come. During his earthly life, Jesus's ministry focused on "the sheep"—on the Jewish nation. This nation did have a special privilege within the working out of God's purposes in history. But the woman's faith in God's mercy overcame such obstacles: "O woman, great is your faith!" (Matt. 15:28).

The Significance of the Miracle

This miracle shows the power of the kingdom of God. And therefore also it shows something about the characteristics of God's kingdom. God's kingdom purpose of salvation starts, indeed, with the Jews. Even Paul, the Apostle to the Gentiles, uses the language "to the Jew first and also to the Greek" (Rom. 1:16). But God's kingdom of salvation also extends to the nations, and even to the most unlikely prospects among them. Salvation comes to people that the first-century Jewish culture would have regarded as less honorable: women, foreigners, pagan idolaters. As Paul writes, the gospel "is the power of God for salvation to *everyone* who believes" (Rom. 1:16). The woman illustrates faith in Christ, and this faith brings salvation. "And he [Christ] came and preached peace to you who were far off and peace to those who were near. For through him we both have access in one Spirit to the Father" (Eph. 2:17–18).

Summary with Clowney's Triangle

We summarize the significance of this miracle with Clowney's triangle (fig. 28.1).

Fig. 28.1: Clowney's Triangle for the Syrophoenician Woman

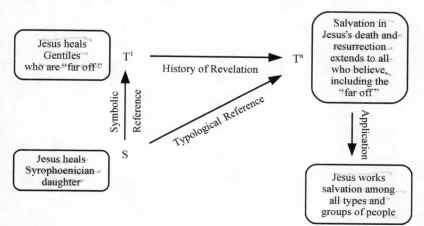

Application

The main application of this miracle is evident: we should understand that Jesus in our day extends salvation to *all* who believe. He does not limit his work to some ethnic groups or language groups or social classes or races or people of privilege.

No one can exclude himself as too unworthy. And no one in the church should dare to make barriers on the basis of ethnicity or social class or "worthiness." We should praise God for the extent of his grace. "All have sinned and fall short of the glory of God" (Rom. 3:23). Counterposed to this universal failure, the invitation of the gospel goes out to all people (Rom. 15:8–13).

29

Healing Many
(Matthew 15:29–31)

Matthew next tells again about the healing of many:

> Jesus went on from there and walked beside the Sea of Galilee. And he went up on the mountain and sat down there. And great crowds came to him, bringing with them the lame, the blind, the crippled, the mute, and many others, and they put them at his feet, and he healed them, so that the crowd wondered, when they saw the mute speaking, the crippled healthy, the lame walking, and the blind seeing. And they glorified the God of Israel. (Matt. 15:29–31)

This description is similar to what is given in the earlier descriptions of many healings (Matt. 4:23–25 [chapter 11]; 9:35–38 [chapter 21]; 12:15–21 [chapter 23]; and 14:34–36 [chapter 27]). We might repeat what we said about them. This description adds detail about what the crowd saw: "they saw the mute speaking, the crippled healthy, the lame walking, and the blind seeing" (Matt. 15:31). In this connection, it brings into prominence one additional aspect, namely the reaction of the crowd. The crowd "wondered" and "they glorified the God of Israel" (v. 31).

In verse 31, we should note how God is described as "the God of
Israel." Within the first-century context, the label "God of Israel"
was more likely to occur on the lips of someone who was *not* a Jew.
From the point of view of a Gentile, God was the God of that *other*
people, the people of Israel, not just "God," as a Jew might say to a
fellow Jew. Accordingly, D. A. Carson and R. T. France think that
the expression "they glorified the God of Israel" indicates that the
episode took place in Gentile territory.[1] Jesus was "beside the Sea
of Galilee" (v. 29). But this might be the *east* side, the region of the
Decapolis, which was predominantly Gentile. If so, this miracle,
like the miracle for the Canaanite woman, points forward to the
time when the gospel will go out to the Gentiles. The same issue
concerning the location and the audience affects the miracle of the
feeding of the 4,000, which comes next (Matt. 15:32–39).

The Significance of the Miracles

These miracles of healing continue the theme of the miracles of the
kingdom of God. But we can add the theme of wonder. Miracles
stimulate the response of wonder, amazement, and awe. People
give glory to God. The reaction of wonder points forward to what
should be our reaction to the climactic miracle in the resurrection of
Christ. When we understand the significance of Jesus's crucifixion,
death, and resurrection, we also respond in wonder and amazement. We can see the pattern of wonder both in Old Testament
prophecy and in Matthew:

> *Who has believed* what he has heard from us?
>> And to whom has the arm of the LORD been revealed?
>> (Isa. 53:1)

> Look among the nations, and see;
>> *wonder and be astounded.*
> For I am doing a work in your days

---

[1] D. A. Carson, "Matthew," in *Expositor's Bible Commentary*, rev. ed., ed. Tremper Longman III and
David E. Garland, vol. 9 (Grand Rapids, MI: Zondervan, 2010), 407; R. T. France, *The Gospel of
Matthew* (Grand Rapids, MI: Eerdmans, 2007), 597.

that you would not *believe* if told.
(Hab. 1:5; cf. Acts 13:41)

When the centurion and those who were with him, keeping watch over Jesus, saw the earthquake and what took place, they were *filled with awe* and said, "Truly this was the Son of God!" (Matt. 27:54)

We can summarize this point using Clowney's triangle (fig. 29.1).

Fig. 29.1: Clowney's Triangle for Wonder at Healings

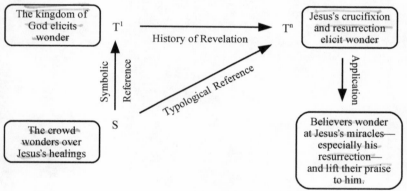

Application of Wonder and Glory

The response to the miracles has an application today. This particular miracle is a special reminder of what should be our response to all the miracles of God. We too should wonder at Jesus's miracles, especially his resurrection. And people in all nations should give glory to "the God of Israel." We give him glory not only for the central miracle of the resurrection of Christ, but also for the miracle of rebirth. This miracle takes place in the heart of each person who is saved, and should be an occasion for giving glory to God and marveling at his grace.

30

Feeding 4,000
(Matthew 15:32–39)

Matthew records the story of Jesus feeding a crowd of 4,000 men (plus women and children):

> Then Jesus called his disciples to him and said, "I have compassion on the crowd because they have been with me now three days and have nothing to eat. And I am unwilling to send them away hungry, lest they faint on the way." And the disciples said to him, "Where are we to get enough bread in such a desolate place to feed so great a crowd?" And Jesus said to them, "How many loaves do you have?" They said, "Seven, and a few small fish." And directing the crowd to sit down on the ground, he took the seven loaves and the fish, and having given thanks he broke them and gave them to the disciples, and the disciples gave them to the crowds. And they all ate and were satisfied. And they took up seven baskets full of the broken pieces left over. Those who ate were four thousand men, besides women and children. And after sending away the crowds, he got into the boat and went to the region of Magadan. (Matt. 15:32–39)

This episode has many parallels with the feeding of the 5,000 in 14:13–21. Its emphasis does not seem to be notably different from the earlier account. So its main thrust is to reemphasize Jesus's care for the people. As with the feeding of the 5,000, physical food symbolizes God's comprehensive care for his people. And this comprehensive care was taking place through the central figure in God's salvation, Jesus the Messiah. We have discussed this significance in our chapter on the feeding of the 5,000 (chapter 25). This second miracle of feeding underscores the fact that Jesus's care for his people continued; it was not given at one time only.

If Carson and France are right about the location being in Gentile territory, the miracle also symbolizes the extension of God's kingdom to the Gentiles. Gentiles also can participate in God's care and eventually will participate in the eschatological banquet (Matt. 8:11).[1]

(For a summary using Clowney's triangle, see fig. 25.1 in chapter 25.)

---

[1] R. T. France, *The Gospel of Matthew* (Grand Rapids, MI: Eerdmans, 2007), 600–601.

31

The Transfiguration
(Matthew 17:1–8)

The story of the transfiguration involves several miraculous elements: Jesus's face and clothes became bright; Moses and Elijah appeared; a bright cloud of theophany overshadowed them; and a voice came from heaven. Here is the account in Matthew 17:1–8:

> And after six days Jesus took with him Peter and James, and John his brother, and led them up a high mountain by themselves. And he was transfigured before them, and his face shone like the sun, and his clothes became white as light. And behold, there appeared to them Moses and Elijah, talking with him. And Peter said to Jesus, "Lord, it is good that we are here. If you wish, I will make three tents here, one for you and one for Moses and one for Elijah." He was still speaking when, behold, a bright cloud overshadowed them, and a voice from the cloud said, "This is my beloved Son, with whom I am well pleased; listen to him." When the disciples heard this, they fell on their faces and were terrified. But Jesus came and touched them, saying, "Rise, and have no fear." And when they lifted up their eyes, they saw no one but Jesus only.

The Significance of the Transfiguration

The transfiguration has several prominent features: the brightness of Jesus, the appearance of Moses and Elijah, and the voice from heaven. The bright appearance of Jesus foreshadows the glory that he received after his resurrection. Indeed, both before and after the passage about the transfiguration come passages in which Jesus predicted his death and resurrection:

> From that time Jesus began to show his disciples that he must go to Jerusalem and suffer many things from the elders and chief priests and scribes, and *be killed*, and on the third day *be raised*. (Matt. 16:21)

> And as they were coming down the mountain, Jesus commanded them, "Tell no one the vision, until the Son of Man is *raised from the dead*." (17:9)

> So also the Son of Man will certainly suffer at their hands. (v. 12)

Thus the transfiguration has a direct link forward to Jesus's glorification, which is tied to the meaning of his resurrection.[1]

We should also consider the meaning of the voice from heaven:

> behold, a bright cloud overshadowed them, and a voice from the cloud said, "This is my beloved Son, with whom I am well pleased; listen to him." (Matt. 17:5)

The message here is similar to the message of God at Jesus's baptism (Matt. 3:17). The voice at the transfiguration speaks the additional words, "Listen to him." That addition has ties with the

---

[1] Note Matthew 16:28: "Truly, I say to you, there are some standing here who will not taste death until they see the Son of Man *coming in his kingdom*." Some interpreters see the fulfillment of this prophecy in the transfiguration, because during the transfiguration Peter and James and John see, by way of foreshadowing, the glory of the Son of Man. This glory expresses his authority as king in the kingdom that will come especially through his resurrection. Others see fulfillment in Jesus's resurrection itself. Still others see fulfillment in the fall of Jerusalem, which does indeed constitute a visible effect of the coming of the reign of the Son of Man in judgment (cf. Matt. 24:27, 30, which I see as having a two-stage fulfillment in the fall of Jerusalem and the second coming). In the light of the central role of the resurrection of Christ, it makes sense to see the primary fulfillment there. But it is also fitting that the transfiguration, which takes place shortly after Jesus's prediction in Matthew 16:28, should function as a nearby pointer to that more distant fulfillment.

conversation that Jesus held with Moses and Elijah: "And behold, there appeared to them Moses and Elijah, *talking* with him" (Matt. 17:3). Moses and Elijah were two great figures in the Old Testament. Both Moses and Elijah had encounters with God on Mount Sinai (also called "Horeb": Ex. 19:19–25; 1 Kings 19:8–18). Matthew 17 indicates that the transfiguration took place on "a high mountain" (v. 1). The coming of the cloud and the voice from the cloud symbolize the coming down of heaven and the voice of God speaking from heaven, which is similar to the voice of God from Mount Sinai, to Moses and later to Elijah. But the voice at the transfiguration said, "Listen to him." That message implies that Jesus is the final prophet whose ministry fulfills and brings to a climax the earlier ministries of Moses and Elijah.

Jesus had much to teach during his earthly life. It looks as though the Gospel of Matthew is organized to highlight his teaching. There are five conspicuous blocks of text that contain his teachings: the Sermon on the Mount (Matthew 5–7), the commissioning of the Twelve (chapter 10), a collection of parables (chapter 13), instructions related to community living (chapter 18), and teaching of a more predictive kind (chapters 21–25). The voice at the transfiguration implies that we should listen to him in all these passages. Then, Matthew 28:19–20 moves the situation forward by referring to this teaching and indicating that the disciples should spread it to the nations:

> Go therefore and *make disciples* of *all nations*, baptizing them in the name of the Father and of the Son and of the Holy Spirit, *teaching them* to observe *all that I have commanded you.* And behold, I am with you always, to the end of the age.

This instruction has its foundation in the authority given to Jesus in his resurrection (Matt. 28:18). So the brightness of light in the transfiguration, anticipating Jesus's resurrection, goes together closely with the voice that tells us to listen. Both point forward to the new phase of the kingdom of God inaugurated by Jesus's resurrection. This new phase then continues to unfold through the spread of the gospel and the discipling of the nations.

Moses and Elijah

We may also note the significance of the appearance of Moses and Elijah. They are both prophets, and their prophetic work points forward to Jesus as the final prophet. But in addition, it is significant that they are alive—their appearance testifies to their ongoing life in the presence of God. Elijah was carried up to heaven without passing through death (2 Kings 2:11). Moses died (Deut. 34:5). The appearance of both of them shows that both are alive according to the spirit. God "is not God of the dead, but of the living, for all live to him" (Luke 20:38). The appearance of Moses and Elijah therefore confirms the life-giving power of God, which is at work for those who are his. It confirms the promise of the bodily resurrection of the saints. It thus reinforces the other ties in Matthew 17:1–8 to the resurrection of Christ. The resurrection of Christ is the firstfruits of the resurrection of the saints (1 Cor. 15:23).

Summary of Significance in Clowney's Triangle

We may summarize the significance of the transfiguration using Clowney's triangle (fig. 31.1).

Fig. 31.1: Clowney's Triangle for the Transfiguration

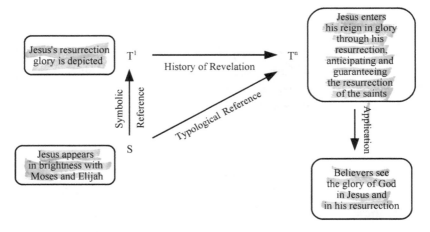

Application

What applications does this miracle have to our lives? The appropriate response to the display of Jesus's glory is to appreciate his glory, and put our trust in him. And as we understand the magnificence and profundity and scope of what Jesus accomplished in his death and resurrection, we grow in faith. We respond in praise and glorify his name.

32

A Boy with a Demon
(Matthew 17:14–20)

Jesus next healed a boy with a demon:

> And when they came to the crowd, a man came up to him and, kneeling before him, said, "Lord, have mercy on my son, for he is an epileptic and he suffers terribly. For often he falls into the fire, and often into the water. And I brought him to your disciples, and they could not heal him." And Jesus answered, "O faithless and twisted generation, how long am I to be with you? How long am I to bear with you? Bring him here to me." And Jesus rebuked the demon, and it came out of him, and the boy was healed instantly. Then the disciples came to Jesus privately and said, "Why could we not cast it out?" He said to them, "Because of your little faith. For truly, I say to you, if you have faith like a grain of mustard seed, you will say to this mountain, 'Move from here to there,' and it will move, and nothing will be impossible for you." (Matt. 17:14–20)

The ESV calls the boy "epileptic" because the symptoms were similar to what we see in modern epilepsy (so also RSV, NRSV). But symptoms may sometimes arise from more than one cause. In this case, a demon was involved.

The Significance of Healing the Boy

This healing appears to have two sides to it. Jesus delivered the boy from the demon. He also healed the boy physically, because the boy had fallen into the fire and into the water. These two sides imply that this miracle goes together both with miracles of exorcism and with miracles of physical healing. As we have seen in discussing exorcisms and physical healings, both kinds of miracles are signs of the kingdom.

What stands out in this case of healing? The passage draws attention to the theme of faith. The disciples were not able to heal the boy "because of your little faith" (Matt. 17:20). So this passage also resonates with other passages that focus on faith, like the healing of the centurion's servant (8:5–13; chapter 13), the woman with a flow of blood (9:18–26; chapter 18), the two blind men (9:27–31; chapter 19), walking on water (14:28–33; chapter 26), and the deliverance of the Syrophoenician woman's daughter (15:21–28; chapter 28). In this case, however, it is the disciples who lacked faith, not the people seeking to be healed.

Summary in Clowney's Triangle

We may summarize the key role of faith using Clowney's triangle (fig. 32.1).

Fig. 32.1: Clowney's Triangle for the Role of Faith in Healing

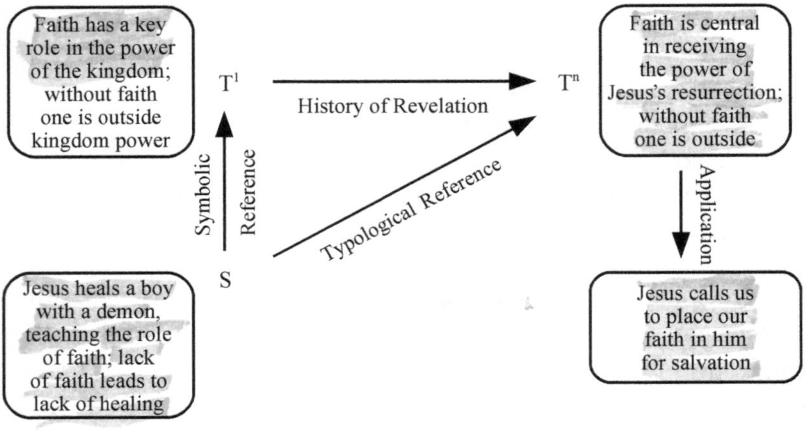

Application

One central application for this story is in encouraging faith. Jesus is the Savior. But we must be united to him to receive the benefits of his salvation. This union takes place by faith. So the story summons us to place our faith in Christ, and in him alone—even the apostles cannot offer an adequate substitute for this faith in Jesus.

33

The Coin in the Fish's Mouth
(Matthew 17:24–27)

A coin was miraculously found in a fish's mouth:

> When they came to Capernaum, the collectors of the two-drachma tax went up to Peter and said, "Does your teacher not pay the tax?" He said, "Yes." And when he came into the house, Jesus spoke to him first, saying, "What do you think, Simon? From whom do kings of the earth take toll or tax? From their sons or from others?" And when he said, "From others," Jesus said to him, "Then the sons are free. However, not to give offense to them, go to the sea and cast a hook and take the first fish that comes up, and when you open its mouth you will find a shekel. Take that and give it to them for me and for yourself." (Matt. 17:24–27)[1]

---

[1] R. T. France interprets this episode as ending, not with a miracle, but with an ironical comment by Jesus (R. T. France, *The Gospel of Matthew* [Grand Rapids, MI: Eerdmans, 2007], 667, 671). France believes that Jesus's comment is not intended to be taken as a literal instruction to Peter, but rather as a comment on the lack of resources in the apostolic band. So, in his view, Peter never went out and found a fish with a coin in its mouth. Is this view correct?

In support of his view, France points out that there are ancient folk stories about finding something valuable in a fish. But the existence of such stories says little about whether Matthew's story is intended as a kind of fictional allusion to these stories or whether it is a real-life analogue to them. Even fictional or exaggerated stories can embody dreams that express longings for redemptive solutions to our difficulties. Over against these dreams, Jesus brings true redemption. So I think we have here a true miracle. It should also be noted that Matthew does not tell

The Significance of the Coin in the Fish's Mouth

Skeptics have expressed their doubts especially in this case concerning the miracle with the coin. This miracle seems to them to be more arbitrary and less related to the broader purposes of the kingdom of God. Instances of healing express Jesus's compassion for the sick and the demoniacs. This miracle seems to be much less helpful, or perhaps even selfish—it just conveniently supplied Jesus and Peter with money, which could less conveniently have been supplied from the common purse (John 12:6).

But a closer look at the episode reveals hints of its significance. This particular episode does not focus on the miracle of the coin but on the discussion that led up to the miracle. "Does your teacher not pay the tax?" (Matt. 17:24). Jesus indicated that Peter and other "sons" of the king are "free." Their status as sons made them free.

Jesus was using an analogy between the kingdom of God and the kingdoms of this world. In the kingdom of God, God is the king and the disciples are his sons. They have the privilege of intimacy with God, and this intimacy supersedes the physical temple and its need for physical maintenance. Jesus himself is the way to God (John 14:6) and the true temple (John 2:21). His name, Immanuel, means "God with us" (Matt. 1:23). The disciples have intimacy with God through him. God "has delivered us from the domain of darkness and transferred us to the kingdom of his beloved Son, in whom we have redemption, the forgiveness of sins" (Col. 1:13–14).

So, concluded Jesus, his disciples, as sons of the kingdom, are "free." But if, to avoid offense, the sons wish to pay anyway, God the king has plenty of resources that he gives to his sons.

The miracle has a double symbolic significance. First, it confirms Jesus's claim that he has a unique status as Son of God. It

about the actual miracle, but breaks the narrative off right after Jesus's speech to Peter. By doing so, the narrative keeps the focus on the theological issue of the status of sons, rather than on the miracle itself.

implies also that his followers through their relationship to him inherit an analogous status. They too are sons, because of their relationship to him. Second, the miracle shows that God can supply *directly* whatever resources are appropriate. "And my God will supply every need of yours according to his riches in glory in Christ Jesus" (Phil. 4:19).

All resources in the world belong to God, theologically speaking. But a miraculous provision from God underscores the privilege of sonship. It displays more vividly the bounty of God's resources and his willingness to supply them to his sons. The lesson is similar to what Jesus gives when telling his disciples to seek first the kingdom of God:

> Therefore do not be anxious, saying, "What shall we eat?" or "What shall we drink?" or "What shall we wear?" For the Gentiles seek after all these things, and your heavenly Father knows that you need them all. But seek first the kingdom of God and his righteousness, and all these things will be added to you. (Matt. 6:31–33)

A dramatic reiteration of this principle was appropriate in the context of the temple tax. The temple was the temple of God. As such, it foreshadowed Christ, whose body is the temple (John 2:21). And subordinately it foreshadows the intimacy with God and access to God that the "sons" of the king receive by virtue of receiving sonship through Jesus the unique Son of God.

The miracle is thus a miracle speaking of divine resources given to the sons of the king of the universe. It anticipates the climactic supply of blessing through the death and resurrection of Christ. The ultimate "resources" are the riches of salvation in Christ.

Summary Using Clowney's Triangle

As usual, we may summarize this significance using Clowney's triangle (fig. 33.1):

Fig. 33.1: Clowney's Triangle for the Coin in the Fish's Mouth

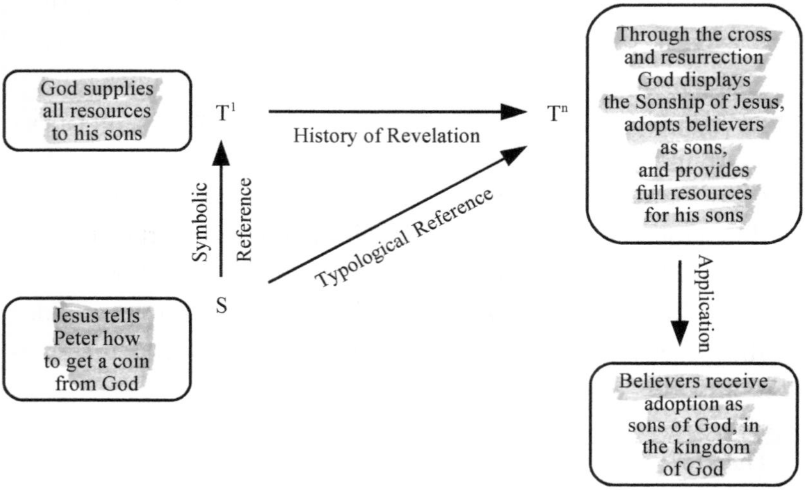

Application

The passage applies to us who have been adopted as sons of God through faith in Jesus. We are sons of the king. We have intimacy with God and an amazing status, not by our own merit but through fellowship with Jesus, who is the unique Son of God:

> But when the fullness of time had come, God sent forth his Son, born of woman, born under the law, to redeem those who were under the law, so that we might receive adoption as sons. And because you are sons, God has sent the Spirit of his Son into our hearts, crying, "Abba! Father!" So you are no longer a slave, but a son, and if a son, then an heir through God. (Gal. 4:4–7)

The passage also implies that those who are still outside of Christ should come to him to become his adopted sons.

34

Many Healings
(Matthew 19:2)

Matthew 19:1–2 offers a summary and a transition that mentions more instances of healing:

> Now when Jesus had finished these sayings, he went away from Galilee and entered the region of Judea beyond the Jordan. And large crowds followed him, and *he healed them* there.

The Significance of Healing

This summary, like the earlier summaries in Matthew, depicts the character of Jesus's ministry of the kingdom of God. His ministry included teaching and miraculous works. Both of these contributed to a total picture. The salvific work of God prophesied in the Old Testament was now unfolding and coming to a climax in Jesus's work. And Jesus's work was leading to his crucifixion and resurrection.

What we have observed about the earlier summary passages in Matthew applies here (see chapter 11 [Matt. 4:23–25]; chapter 14 [Matt. 8:14–17]; chapter 21 [Matt. 9:35–38]; chapter 23 [Matt. 12:15–21]; chapter 27 [Matt. 14:34–36]; chapter 29 [Matt.

15:29–31]). Jesus was on his way to Jerusalem and his final days. So a final summary of the larger scope of his work is appropriate at this point in the narrative of Matthew.

(For a summary using Clowney's triangle, see fig. 11.1 in chapter 11.)

35

Two Blind Men at Jericho
(Matthew 20:29–34)

Jesus healed two blind men at Jericho:

> And as they went out of Jericho, a great crowd followed him.
> And behold, there were two blind men sitting by the roadside,
> and when they heard that Jesus was passing by, they cried out,
> "Lord, have mercy on us, Son of David!" The crowd rebuked
> them, telling them to be silent, but they cried out all the more,
> "Lord, have mercy on us, Son of David!" And stopping, Jesus
> called them and said, "What do you want me to do for you?"
> They said to him, "Lord, let our eyes be opened." And Jesus in
> pity touched their eyes, and immediately they recovered their
> sight and followed him. (Matt. 20:29–34)

The Significance of Healing

This story of healing is similar to the earlier healing of two blind
men in Matthew 9:27–31 (see chapter 19). As in the earlier episode,
the blind men called Jesus "Son of David" (20:30, 31), thereby
bringing into focus his messianic status. This healing at Jericho
is followed immediately by the triumphal entry (Matt. 21:1–11),

which Matthew explicitly links with messianic fulfillment of Zechariah 9:9 (Matt. 21:4–5). The crowd greeted Jesus with the shout, "Hosanna to the *Son of David*! Blessed is he who comes in the name of the Lord! Hosanna in the highest!" (Matt. 21:9). Like the earlier miracle of healing two blind men, this instance of healing signifies the restoration not merely of physical sight but of spiritual sight as well. Spiritual sight results in recognizing Jesus as the Messiah.

Fittingly, the two blind men who had been healed "followed him" (Matt. 20:34). Matthew does not say explicitly that the two men followed him all the way from Jericho to Bethphage and Jerusalem. But thematically their response to Jesus is linked to the welcome from the crowds. Both the blind men and the crowds recognized that Jesus was "the Son of David." However, in the case of the crowds we have to say that their "recognition" was partial and fickle. They understood the true nature of Jesus's messianic work even less than the twelve apostles.

Why does Matthew record two separate instances of healing two blind men, when the two miracles have much the same significance? The effect of having two episodes with so many similarities is like the effect of having two miracles of multiplying loaves and fish, one with 5,000 men and the other with 4,000 (Matt. 14:13–21 and 15:32–39; see also chapters 25 and 30). Reiteration reinforces the point. In the case of the two blind men, the healing at Jericho took place as Jesus was on his final journey to Jerusalem. It is fitting that we have a final miracle with messianic significance and with significance for spiritual sight just before the triumphal entry, and just before Jesus went through the events of climactic messianic significance, in the cross and resurrection.

As usual, we can apply the passage to our lives. We receive spiritual sight when Jesus gives us sight through the Holy Spirit.

Summary Using Clowney's Triangle

The summary using Clowney's triangle is essentially the same as with the earlier instance of healing two blind men (fig. 35.1).

Fig. 35.1: Clowney's Triangle for the Two Blind Men at Jericho

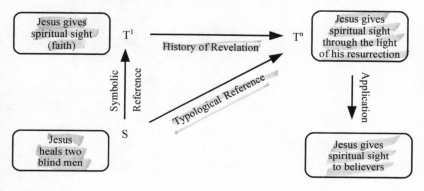

36

Cursing the Fig Tree
(Matthew 21:18–22)

A fig tree miraculously withered after Jesus cursed it:

> In the morning, as he was returning to the city, he became
> hungry. And seeing a fig tree by the wayside, he went to it and
> found nothing on it but only leaves. And he said to it, "May
> no fruit ever come from you again!" And the fig tree withered
> at once.
>
> When the disciples saw it, they marveled, saying, "How did
> the fig tree wither at once?" And Jesus answered them, "Truly,
> I say to you, if you have faith and do not doubt, you will not
> only do what has been done to the fig tree, but even if you say
> to this mountain, 'Be taken up and thrown into the sea,' it will
> happen. And whatever you ask in prayer, you will receive, if you
> have faith." (Matt. 21:18–22)

This miracle has proved difficult for some readers. The first difficulty lies in the relation of Matthew to Mark. Mark records the
same events in a somewhat different way (Mark 11:12–14, 20–25).
In comparison to Mark, Matthew has chosen to give a compressed
account. For a discussion of the harmony between the accounts,

in the midst of the differences, one may see my *Inerrancy and the Gospels.*[1]

A second difficulty arises because it seems to some readers that Jesus was overly severe with the fig tree. The fig tree was only a tree, not a person. Why did he curse it?

We must understand that what we have here is a prophetic action, like an acted-out parable. The episode with the fig tree stands right next to the episode where Jesus cleansed the temple (Matt. 21:12–17). Jesus cleansed the temple because the traders had corrupted it (vv. 12–13). Israel as a nation was "planted" by God in the land of Palestine in order that it might bear fruit in good works. Isaiah's parable of the vineyard (Isa. 5:1–7) and Ezekiel's parable of the vine (Ezek. 19:10–14) both set up parallels between Israel and fruit-bearing. The need to cleanse the temple was one symptom of the fact that, in Jesus's time, Israel as a corporate nation was not bearing proper spiritual fruit.

The parallel between Israel and this fruitless fig tree is more striking because of a particular feature of fig trees. Characteristically, the leaves and the fruit of a fig tree grow together. From a distance, Jesus saw that the fig tree had leaves. The leaves seemed to promise that it would also have fruit. But it did not. Similarly, Israel's status as the Old Testament people of God, together with the care that God had lavished upon her, seemed to promise that Israel, above any other nation, would show fruit in righteousness. But close inspection showed that she did not live up to her promise.

In fact, the issue is more subtle. Not all within Israel stood equally under judgment. The trouble with the fig tree was not merely that it did not have fruit, but that its display of leaves seemed to promise fruit. The fig tree is thus a symbol for human hypocrisy. So Jesus's acted-out parable fits together with his criticism of the religious leaders in Israel. It serves as a warning to all who profess religion but do not bring forth fruit.[2]

---

[1] Vern S. Poythress, *Inerrancy and the Gospels: A God-Centered Approach to the Challenges of Harmonization* (Wheaton, IL: Crossway, 2012), chapter 20.

[2] D. A. Carson, "Matthew," in *Expositor's Bible Commentary*, rev. ed., ed. Tremper Longman III and David E. Garland, vol. 9 (Grand Rapids, MI: Zondervan, 2010), 502–503.

Because of the parallels here, we can see that Jesus's action toward the fig tree had a message for Israel. It was not *merely* about being frustrated over a fig tree. Jesus's action, as we observed, was *prophetic* action, warning of the curse of God that would fall on Israelites unless they repented and bore fruit. This message of warning and call to repentance began even with John the Baptist:

> But when he saw many of the Pharisees and Sadducees coming to his baptism, he said to them, "You brood of vipers! Who warned you to flee from the wrath to come? *Bear fruit* in keeping with repentance. And do not presume to say to yourselves, 'We have Abraham as our father,' for I tell you, God is able from these stones to raise up children for Abraham. Even now the axe is laid to the root of the trees. Every tree therefore that does not *bear good fruit* is cut down and thrown into the fire. (Matt. 3:7–10)

The Significance of Cursing the Fig Tree

So what is the significance of this miracle of Jesus? It symbolizes a warning to all in Israel that they must bear fruit. Especially, it focused on the leaders of the Jews. If they did not repent, they would wither, be cut down, and be thrown into the fire.

Such is the nature of the kingdom of God. God comes to bring salvation. But accompanying his salvation is purification and judgment on all that stands opposed to him and his righteousness. It was tempting for individual Jews and especially for the leaders to try to rely on their privileged position as descendants of Abraham. Thus John the Baptist warned, "And do not presume to say to yourselves, 'We have Abraham as our father,' for I tell you, God is able from these stones to raise up children for Abraham" (Matt. 3:9).

The warning of judgment against the Jewish leaders came to its climax with the crucifixion and the resurrection. The Jewish leaders actively worked to bring about Jesus's crucifixion. And in this they were acting as archenemies of God, bringing down a judgment on themselves that finally took place visibly in the fall of Jerusalem in

AD 70. At the same time, the challenge comes to every individual Jew: what will you do with Jesus? Whose son is he? What is the significance of his crucifixion? Was it *merely* the death of one more disgraced criminal? Or was it the working out of God's plan to save:

> This Jesus, delivered up according to the definite plan and foreknowledge of God, you crucified and killed by the hands of lawless men. God raised him up, loosing the pangs of death, because it was not possible for him to be held by it. (Acts 2:23–24)

Jesus himself bore the curse that should fall on sinners. He was forsaken by God in order that God might not bring forsakenness on us: "My God, my God, why have you *forsaken me*?" (Matt. 27:46). He laid down his life in ransom, in order that many might be ransomed: "The Son of Man came not to be served but to serve, and to *give his life* as a *ransom for many*" (Matt. 20:28). Those Jews and Gentiles who recognize the saving significance of the crucifixion trust in Jesus and bear fruit. The rest do not, and as a result their lives wither. They remain cut off from the source of eternal life in Christ.

Applications

The warning about fruitlessness applies to hearers today. Our response to the message of Christ's crucifixion and resurrection involves either belief or unbelief. Believing in Christ leads to fruit. Unbelief leads to fruitlessness and curse.

Summary Using Clowney's Triangle

We offer a summary of the significance of the fig tree using Clowney's triangle (fig. 36.1).

Fig. 36.1: Clowney's Triangle for the Cursing of the Fig Tree

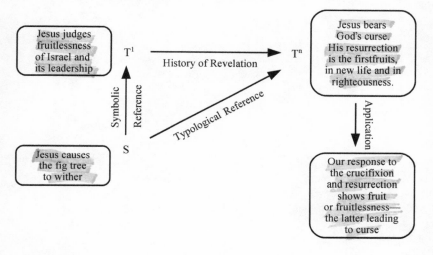

Part IV

THE RESURRECTION
OF CHRIST AND
ITS APPLICATION

37

The Resurrection of Jesus
(Matthew 28:1–10)

The culminating miracle in the book of Matthew consists in the resurrection of Jesus. It was announced by angels and confirmed by the appearance of Jesus himself:

> Now after the Sabbath, toward the dawn of the first day of the week, Mary Magdalene and the other Mary went to see the tomb. And behold, there was a great earthquake, for an angel of the Lord descended from heaven and came and rolled back the stone and sat on it. His appearance was like lightning, and his clothing white as snow. And for fear of him the guards trembled and became like dead men. But the angel said to the women, "Do not be afraid, for I know that you seek Jesus who was crucified. He is not here, for he has risen, as he said. Come, see the place where he lay. Then go quickly and tell his disciples that he has risen from the dead, and behold, he is going before you to Galilee; there you will see him. See, I have told you."
> So they departed quickly from the tomb with fear and great joy, and ran to tell his disciples. And behold, Jesus met them and said, "Greetings!" And they came up and took hold of his feet and worshiped him. Then Jesus said to them, "Do not be

afraid; go and tell my brothers to go to Galilee, and there they will see me." (Matt. 28:1–10)

The mention of Galilee points forward to the meeting in Galilee where Jesus issued the Great Commission (Matt. 28:16–20). The miracle of Christ's resurrection has a close relationship to the Great Commission. It leads to the Great Commission, not only because Jesus summoned his disciples to go to Galilee, but because the Great Commission has its foundation in Jesus's universal authority: "All authority in heaven and on earth has been given to me" (v. 18). This authority was invested in Jesus by virtue of his resurrection (cf. Phil. 2:9–11).

The Significance of the Resurrection

So what is the significance of the resurrection? The preceding miracles in the Gospel of Matthew have significance in pointing forward to the resurrection of Christ. The resurrection of Christ is itself the "capstone" to which they point forward. It has significance in itself. It is not primarily a pointer to something else.

Yet even the resurrection of Christ does not stand in isolation from God's larger plan for history. Christ was raised not merely as a benefit to Christ himself in his human nature, but as a benefit to all those who belong to him, those who are "in Christ." Romans 6 and Colossians 3:1–4 both indicate how Christians receive new life, resurrection life, from Christ:

> Do you not know that all of us who have been baptized into Christ Jesus were baptized into his death? We were buried therefore with him by baptism into death, in order that, just as Christ was *raised* from the dead by the glory of the Father, we too might walk *in newness of life.*
>
> For if we have been united with him in a death like his, we shall certainly be *united with him in a resurrection like his.* . . . Now if we have died with Christ, we believe that we will also *live with him.* . . . So you also must consider yourselves dead to sin and *alive to God in Christ Jesus.* . . . Do not present your

members to sin as instruments for unrighteousness, but present yourselves to God as those who have been *brought from death to life*, and your members to God as instruments for righteousness. (Rom. 6:3–5, 8, 11, 13)

If then you have been raised with Christ, seek the things that are above, where Christ is, seated at the right hand of God. Set your minds on things that are above, not on things that are on earth. For you have died, and your life is hidden with Christ in God. When Christ who is your life appears, then you also will appear with him in glory. (Col. 3:1–4)

The resurrection of Christ was also the beginning of a whole new world. Christ in his resurrection body belongs to a whole order of existence permanently free from the power of death: "We know that Christ, being raised from the dead, will *never* die again; death no longer has dominion over him. For the death he died he died to sin, once for all, but the life he lives he lives to God" (Rom. 6:9–10). His physical body is therefore the first portion of a whole new world. In his resurrection he himself inaugurated the new heaven and new earth.

When the entire new heaven and new earth come, as described in Revelation 21:1–22:5, the new world will participate in "the freedom of the glory of the children of God" (Rom. 8:21). The pattern for its liberation is the freedom of the children of God. And their freedom comes in accordance with the pattern established by Christ's resurrection. Thus, Christ's resurrection is the centerpiece and foundation for the resurrection of the bodies of believers (1 Cor. 15:44–49) and the renewal of the whole creation order. It is the very fulcrum of history.

The Old Testament has anticipations and foreshadowings of Christ's resurrection. For example, we may think of Enoch, who was taken up to God without passing through death (Gen. 5:24). Or consider Noah. Noah and his family came through the waters of the flood and entered a new world, cleansed of wickedness. Joseph went to prison, a kind of living death, and then was rescued and exalted according to the plan of God. The Israelites obtained new life when they came out of bondage in Egypt. In the crossing of the Red Sea they went down, symbolically speaking, into the waters of death and came up on the other side, entering into new life. The New Testament makes explicit one kind of analogy between the Red Sea crossing and Christian redemption when it speaks about the Israelites being "baptized into Moses in the cloud and in the sea" (1 Cor. 10:2)—a parallel to Christian baptism, which symbolizes new life in Christ.

The widow of Zarephath's son was brought back to life by Elijah (1 Kings 17:17–24), and the Shunammite's son by Elisha (2 Kings 4:32–37). Daniel was raised up from the lions' den (Dan. 6:23). Jonah came up out of the depths of the sea, which symbolized death (Jonah 2:6, 10). In his own earthly ministry, Jesus raised Jairus's daughter and Lazarus.

All these episodes show God giving new life in one form or another. But they are all still preliminary. The transition to existence permanently free from death comes only through Christ's triumph over death:

> Since therefore the children share in flesh and blood, he himself likewise partook of the same things, that through death he might destroy the one who has the power of death, that is, the devil, and deliver all those who through fear of death were subject to lifelong slavery. (Heb. 2:14–15)

> Fear not, I am the first and the last, and the living one. I died, and behold I am *alive forevermore*, and I have the keys of Death and Hades. (Rev. 1:17–18)

We who belong to Christ live even now with the eternal life that he has given us through the indwelling Holy Spirit. We look forward to the completion of his triumph over death when death is swallowed up forever:

> He will swallow up death forever;
> and the Lord GOD will wipe away tears from all faces,

and the reproach of his people he will take away from all
   the earth,
for the LORD has spoken. (Isa. 25:8)

And I heard a loud voice from the throne saying, "Behold, the
dwelling place of God is with man. He will dwell with them,
and they will be his people, and God himself will be with them
as their God. He will wipe away every tear from their eyes, and
death shall be no more, neither shall there be mourning, nor
crying, nor pain anymore, for the former things have passed
away." (Rev. 21:3–4)

He who testifies to these things says, "Surely I am coming
soon." Amen. Come, Lord Jesus! (Rev. 22:20)

The Great Commission

As we already observed, in the narrative in Matthew the resurrection leads to the Great Commission, given in Matthew 28:18–20.
The Great Commission begins with an announcement of Jesus's
universal authority: "all authority in heaven and on earth has
been given to me" (v. 18). The fact that Jesus has received authority is an implication of his resurrection, and the resurrection is a
demonstration of Christ's Sonship. Baptism, according to Matthew 28:19, is "in the name of the Father and of the Son and of
the Holy Spirit." The inclusion of the Son along with the Father
and the Spirit presupposes the deity of the Son. The formula for
baptism compresses into a short form the doctrine of the Trinity, as it would later be worked out explicitly in the course of
theological reflection in the church. Jesus is God as well as exalted Son of Man. So the resurrection underscores what earlier
miracles in Matthew indicated: Christ's deity and his messianic
role as Redeemer.

    Christ's redemption now needs to extend throughout the world,
as people hear the gospel, believe, receive baptism, and grow as
disciples.

The Rending of the Temple Curtain
and the Raising of Dead Saints

Let us also look briefly at the miracles recorded in Matthew 27:51–53. They further underscore the significance of Jesus's resurrection. There are three miracles in a cluster. In the first miracle, "the curtain of the temple was torn in two, from top to bottom" (v. 51). The reference is probably to the inner curtain in the temple, the curtain that separated the Most Holy Place from the Holy Place. This curtain signified that the way into the innermost presence of God was barred to human access (Heb. 9:8). God is holy, while the people are unholy. Hence, they cannot enter the presence of God (cf. Isa. 6:5). According to the law of Moses, even the high priest, who is consecrated and holy on a symbolic level, can enter the Most Holy Place only once a year, on the Day of Atonement, taking with him the blood of the atonement (Leviticus 16; Heb. 9:7).

Thus, the rending of the curtain indicates that Christ has opened the way into the presence of God. He opens the way to God's presence in heaven, not merely the Most Holy Place on earth, which is symbolic of his presence on earth (Heb. 10:20). The fact that the rending starts from the top, rather than the bottom, indicates that the opening is accomplished by God, not man.

The second miracle contained in the cluster in Matthew 27:51–53 consists in the earthquake and the splitting of rocks: "And the earth shook, and the rocks were split" (v. 51). The earthquake was a manifestation of the power of God, reminiscent of the shaking of the earth when God appeared at Mount Sinai (Ex. 19:18). This exhibition of power underscores the power involved in Christ's death and resurrection.

The third miracle consists in raising dead saints: "The tombs also were opened. And many bodies of the saints who had fallen asleep were raised, and coming out of the tombs after his resurrection they went into the holy city and appeared to many" (vv. 52–53). Note that the appearances took place "after his resurrection." The raising of some of the saints underscores the fact that Christ's resurrection has significance not only for him personally but for all the saints. Their resurrection is guaranteed by his. We know from other parts of the Bible that the worldwide resurrection of the saints takes place when Christ returns (1 Thess. 4:13–18; see also 1 Cor. 15:23). But Matthew 27:52–53 indicates that a smaller group of saints were raised at an earlier point. This event pictures on a small scale what will happen at the second coming. Both the small-scale event and the future resurrection of the saints have their foundation in the resurrection of Christ.

38

Applications to
Particular Needs

The resurrection of Christ was a unique event that took place at a particular time in the first century AD, at a particular place, the tomb of Joseph of Arimathea. It is an unrepeatable event. At the same time, it is an event with universal relevance, because it forms the foundation for the spiritual transformation of all people in union with Christ. This transformation takes place once and for all at the time of initial repentance and conversion to Christ through the Holy Spirit. But continual transformation also takes place, day by day (Rom. 12:1–2). And at the time of the second coming the resurrection of Christ issues in the physical, bodily resurrection of believers, and their entrance into a new heaven and a new earth that follow the pattern of Christ's resurrection (Rom. 8:18–25).

Universal Relevance of Miracles

Throughout this book we have stressed that the miracles of Jesus are signs of redemption; and this redemption came to a climax in Jesus's resurrection. Since the resurrection has universal relevance, the miracles as signs also have universal relevance, because of their tie to the resurrection. The miracle stories have applications throughout this gospel age and, in addition, to the final resurrection of the body and the coming of the new heaven and new earth. For similar reasons, the same can also be said concerning the miracles and types in the Old Testament.

Relevance to Human Struggles

By implication, the miracles have relevance to particular situations that crop up in people's lives. In chapter 8 we considered Joe, who is bored doing dishes. Likewise, Sue is disciplining her son; Dave is depressed by failure; and Jane is elated with romance. The miracles of Jesus are relevant to each of these situations.

For a person who is in a struggle, *one* miracle may sometimes speak more vividly than another. For example, the miracle at Cana in Galilee took place at a wedding, and foreshadows the feast at the marriage supper of the Lamb (Rev. 19:9). Because of the wedding theme, it is possible that it may speak more vividly and vitally to Jane, who is filled with interest in a possible budding romance. It may remind her that desires for earthly pleasure need to be set in the context of God's plan, which includes earthly blessings but does not end with them. God's plan subordinates temporary pleasures to the deepest pleasure of final communion with God, as represented in the marriage supper of the Lamb.

The stories of miracles are pertinent to people in all circumstances, whether they are elated or struggling or distressed. They are also pertinent to any friend who wants to encourage someone in distress, and to professional counselors who have many people coming to them in distress. Suppose Holly is in distress. She needs encouragement from the Bible about God and his ways, and understanding of how God works with people in distress. The stories in the Bible complement the passages that teach explicitly about God's providential care.

Consider a particular situation. Nancy finds that she cannot shake off the feeling of being "dirty." She feels dirty because she has been the victim of sexual abuse. Or maybe she feels dirty because she has freely consented to immoral sexual relations. The story of the healing of the leper in Matthew 8:1–4 can speak powerfully to her because the leper is a person who is socially "dirty" (unclean) by the standards of society and indeed by the standards of the symbolism in the Mosaic law. Nancy considers this particular miracle story and thinks about the analogies between it and her life. And then she can move from the particular miracle to the climactic miracle of Jesus's death and resurrection. Nancy can grow in seeing the relevance of Jesus's resurrection to her situation. Nancy can be made clean as she comes to Jesus. Second Corinthians 5:17 says, "If anyone is in Christ, he is a new creation." Nancy needs to appreciate that Christ has gone down under sin and death, for her sake, and has then come up in the resurrection in order that she may live a new life, renewed day by day. Forgiveness of sin and healing from victimization come from Jesus.

Consider another situation. Mary is grieving over the news that her mother is dying of cancer. She is concerned for a person she loves, not for herself. The miracle of the healing of the centurion's servant or the healing of Peter's mother-in-law is relevant to her (Matt. 8:5–13, 14–17). The Bible indicates God does not always answer our prayers by healing immediately (2 Cor. 12:9; 2 Tim. 4:20). But prayer for healing is certainly legitimate, and the conviction that God *can* heal through Christ is well-founded. As the centurion says, "only say the word, and my servant will be healed" (Matt. 8:8). Healing comes either immediately, or later in this life, or still later in the resurrection of the body. Mary may come to see the relevance of one or two miracle stories to her situation. She may then be able to move from there to see the relevance of the great miracle, namely Jesus's resurrection. She may also receive help from passages that talk about trials:

> Count it all joy, my brothers, when you meet trials of various kinds, for you know that the testing of your faith produces

steadfastness. And let steadfastness have its full effect, that you may be perfect and complete, lacking in nothing. (James 1:2–4)

Tammy is overwhelmed with demands and busyness, in which she says she is "drowning." So the miracle when Jesus stills the storm (Matt. 8:23–27) is relevant to her. If she sees its relevance, she can—just like Nancy or Mary—travel from the miracle of stilling the storm to the miracle of Jesus's resurrection.

Don feels as if he is going to go crazy. The pressures on his job tempt him to scream. Or maybe he has troubling thoughts, telling him to commit suicide, or he hears voices telling him to commit terrible crimes. Would Don see an analogy between the Gadarene demoniacs and his situation? His situation may be bad, and his thoughts may be terrifying, but he may still be able to see that he has not yet moved into a life as terrible as the demoniacs. If Jesus can deliver the demoniacs, he can also deliver Don. As usual, the miracle of delivering the demoniacs points to the greatest miracle, the miracle of Jesus's resurrection.

These specific examples have connections with many didactic passages:

No temptation has overtaken you that is not common to man. God is faithful, and he will not let you be tempted beyond your ability, but with the temptation he will also provide the way of escape, that you may be able to endure it. (1 Cor. 10:13)

I can do all things through him who strengthens me. (Phil. 4:13)

Submit yourselves therefore to God. Resist the devil, and he will flee from you. (James 4:7)

George feels paralyzed by guilt. He can't move on in life. So consider how the miracle of healing the paralytic (Matt. 9:1–8) speaks to him. Christ can heal his spiritual paralysis through his resurrection: "There is therefore now no condemnation for those who are in Christ Jesus" (Rom. 8:1).

Judy is deeply depressed. She walks through her day like a zombie, feeling that all interest in life is gone and she is as good as dead. Could she see the relevance of the story of the raising of Jairus's daughter (Matt. 9:18–26)? Or consider the story of the raising of Lazarus (John 11:1–44).

> Why are you cast down, O my soul,
> > and why are you in turmoil within me?
> Hope in God; for I shall again praise him,
> > my salvation and my God. (Ps. 42:11)

These instances from people's lives illustrate how wide-ranging are the applications arising from the miracle stories about Jesus. (See fig. 38.1.)

Fig. 38.1: Applications from the Miracle Stories about Jesus

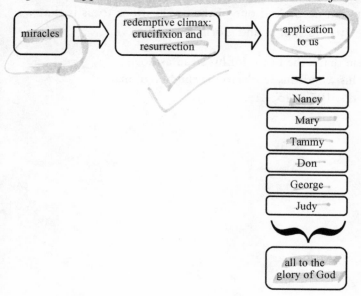

Sensitivity and Selectivity

If one story from the Bible does not make an impression on Judy, it is still possible that another will. The Gospels are full of miracle stories. We have illustrated using miracle stories from John and

Matthew. But the same principles hold for Mark and Luke. And in a still broader way, the same hold for redemptive plots throughout the Bible. They all have power to speak to people who feel distressed or guilty or trapped or faced with death. The word of God has divine power. But it is also true that the Holy Spirit must work to bring that power to bear on those who suffer. People in distress and those who are trying to encourage them should be praying that the Holy Spirit will show them a story or stories through which the Spirit will speak vividly and powerfully, and bring new life in Christ to those who suffer.

No human being has the power to change the heart. Only God does. He has demonstrated that power in the miracles of Jesus. And he continues to demonstrate that power as he applies the healing of Jesus's death and resurrection to all kinds of situations of human sin and human need. And one of the applications to us is that we are enabled to praise him and glorify his name:

> Let them thank the LORD for his steadfast love,
> for his wondrous works to the children of man.
>   (Ps. 107:8, 15, 21, 31)

Conclusion

We have completed our journey through the miracles recorded in the Gospel of Matthew. They are indeed signs of redemption. They show the power of God, the power of kingdom, and the lordship of Jesus who is the king of the kingdom and the divine Son of God. But in addition they foreshadow that great central work of Jesus in his crucifixion, death, resurrection, and ascension. By pointing to Jesus, they also proclaim the gospel in its various aspects.

May the miracles serve, then, to show the gospel again in its freshness. And may the Holy Spirit continue through the message of the gospel to open eyes that are spiritually blind and give new life to people who are spiritually dead. May people from all nations become disciples and rejoice in Christ and his salvation.

Christ's redemption has accomplished everything we need. And so it finds application not only in each individual at the time of conversion, but in daily living as well. May the miracles in the Gospels continue to speak to people like Joe who are bored while washing dishes, to people like Sue who are disciplining their children, to people like Dave who are depressed by failure in school, and to people like Jane who are elated with anticipation of romance. May the miracles speak to those in every kind of sin, distress, and trouble—people who need the healing plot of redemption operating in their own lives, both in regeneration and in daily living. May people continue to experience Christ's redemption worked out in their lives. May they lift up their voices to praise and glorify

God, as they see his "wondrous works to the children of man" (Ps. 107:8).

God has designed the miracles in the Gospels with these purposes in mind, as well as the more obvious purposes—telling us what happened, telling us that Jesus is the Messiah and Savior, and confirming the claims about Christ with astonishing works in time and space.

Appendix

Miracles in the Whole Bible

We have explored how the miracles recorded in John and in Matthew offer analogues to the climactic acts of redemption in the crucifixion and resurrection of Christ. If such is true for the miracles in John and in Matthew, is it also true for Mark and for Luke? Yes. The same kinds of reasoning work for all four Gospels. As previously noted, Richard Phillips has written a book that applies these principles to the Gospel of Luke.[1]

The Analogies within the Gospels

May we extend the same principles beyond the confines of the four Gospels? Consider again the healing of the leper in Matthew 8:1–4 (see chapter 12). Drawing a line from the healing of the leper to the crucifixion and the resurrection makes sense partly because Matthew as a whole gives us a continuous narrative that leads from one to the other. In addition, the theme of the coming of the kingdom of God unites all the events that Matthew records. Moreover, Jesus himself is the central actor both in healing the leper and in the final events of crucifixion and resurrection. He is himself the central link uniting the two. The same links are present in Mark and Luke, so

[1] Richard D. Phillips, *Mighty to Save: Discovering God's Grace in the Miracles of Jesus* (Phillipsburg, NJ: Presbyterian & Reformed, 2001).

we can infer that there too the miracles function as signs of redemption, pointing forward to the cross and the resurrection.

Analogies in Acts

Can the same principles be applied in the book of Acts? The miracles in the book of Acts take place by the power of the Holy Spirit, and accompany the preaching of the gospel. They presuppose the fact of Christ's resurrection, his ascension, and the pouring out of the Holy Spirit at Pentecost. The gospel that is proclaimed in Acts is the gospel announcing the death and resurrection of Christ, in fulfillment of the Old Testament Scriptures.

The gospel in the book of Acts fundamentally points backward to the events of redemption that Christ has already accomplished. At the same time, it calls on people to respond in faith to Christ, to respond to who he is and what he has done. The miracles are redemptive deeds that go alongside the redemptive announcement of the gospel. They reinforce the message of the gospel. Thus, though they come after Christ's resurrection rather than before, they have a function similar to the miracles during Christ's earthly life. They testify to the kingdom of God, and they reveal the nature of that kingdom. They are signs of redemption. They are miniature pictures, then, of the redemption that Christ brings through his resurrection and through the coming of the Holy Spirit.

Miracles in the Old Testament

Do the miracles in the Old Testament function as signs of redemption? We may not always find that the connections forward to Christ are quite as striking as with the miracles that Christ himself performed while he was on earth. But the idea of miracles foreshadowing the work of Christ still has force.[2]

One of the most outstanding clusters of miracles in the Old Testament occurs in the exodus from Egypt. The exodus includes a

---

[2] I have also discussed the general principles for understanding redemptive plots in Vern S. Poythress, *In the Beginning Was the Word: Language—A God-Centered Approach* (Wheaton, IL: Crossway, 2009), chapters 24–26.

whole series of miracles: the ten plagues, the crossing of the Red Sea, and the appearance of God on Mount Sinai. Together, these miracles brought about redemption from Egypt. And redemption from Egypt is clearly a *type* or foreshadowing of redemption in Christ. For example, 1 Corinthians 5:7 points out an analogy between the Passover at the time of the exodus and Christ "our Passover Lamb." First Corinthians 10:2 points out an analogy between crossing the Red Sea and Christian baptism. Hebrews 3:1–6 points out an analogy between Moses and Christ. We could cite many such passages.

Likewise Noah's flood was a miracle of judgment and redemption. The wicked were judged, and Noah and his family were saved. First Peter 3:20–21 makes an analogy between Noah's flood and Christian salvation, as symbolized by baptism.

In addition, in previous chapters we have pointed to some analogies between Christ's miracles and those of Elijah and Elisha.

We should not be surprised by these analogies, because the whole Old Testament points forward to Christ, as Christ himself indicated in Luke 24:25–27, 44–47. The prophets like Moses, Elijah, and Elisha point forward to Christ the final prophet (Heb. 1:1–3). In the Gospels, the expression "the kingdom of God" or "the kingdom of heaven" designates the saving work of God during the climax of history, in fulfillment of Old Testament prophecy. But in the broader sense God was at work as king in saving people all the way through the Old Testament. So the expression "kingdom of God" can be expanded to encompass miraculous works of salvation in the Old Testament.

In Luke 24:44–47 Christ taught his disciples that the Old Testament is about him. This idea is not a new invention by Christ. Rather, Christ was saying that the Old Testament was *always* about him, even before the time when he came into the world. God was speaking about redemption in the Old Testament. God gave the people instances of redemption, like the redemption from Egypt. These acts of redemption anticipated the final act of redemption in Christ. God intended from the beginning that his words and deeds in the Old Testament should demonstrate grace, and that grace was always based on Christ's achievement, though the achievement itself—his life, death, and resurrection—was still in the future during the time of the Old Testament. From the beginning, God designed the Old Testament to have its significance in relation to Christ who was still to come. This principle is illustrated in the Old Testament covenants: God made covenants with his people, and the covenants anticipate the new covenant inaugurated by Christ (Mark 14:24; 1 Cor. 11:25).[3]

Thus, the meaning that God gave to his people in Old Testament times has an organic coherence with the meaning that we can perceive now. God's communication was dimly understood in the past; we understand it more clearly now.

And, why confine ourselves to *miraculous* works? In Scripture, God works through ordinary providential means as well as in miracles. His ordinary providence is less spectacular, but in the end just as effective. When Saul was pursuing David to kill him, David was repeatedly delivered. Circumstances conspired against Saul, we might say. But the circumstances were of course under God's control. It was God who delivered David. Near the end of his life, David explicitly recognized this: "As the LORD lives, who has redeemed my soul out of every adversity . . ." (1 Kings 1:29).

In speaking of "every adversity," David was focusing to some extent on various *physical* adversities, not simply spiritual trials. But the deliverances from these physical adversities demonstrated God's love and care for David. And God's love and care extend to every aspect of life, not just the physical side. In the Psalms of David, we can see how God took care of David's emotional and spiritual struggles, not simply his needs for physical deliverance. In sum, God's acts of deliverance, whether miraculous or providential, serve as signs of redemption, and small acts of redemption look forward to *comprehensive* redemption, which God has achieved through Christ.

---

[3] For a fuller explanation, see "Overview of the Bible: A Survey of the History of Salvation," in *The ESV Study Bible* (Wheaton, IL: Crossway, 2008), 23–26, http://www.frame-poythress.org/overview-of-the-bible-a-survey-of-the-history-of-salvation/, accessed July 3, 2014.

Fig. A.1 summarizes the way in which redemption in Christ has relationships to all the rest of the Bible.

Fig. A.1: The Centrality of Christ in the Bible

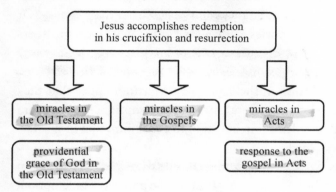

Types and Typology

In our examination of the miracles in John and Matthew, we have repeatedly used Clowney's triangle in order to appreciate the symbolic significance of miracles. But Clowney originally produced his triangle to express his ideas for how to interpret Old Testament *types*. So an analysis of Old Testament miracles can take place by using the ideas summarized in Clowney's triangle, and bringing them to bear on the Old Testament—the very place where Clowney originally intended the triangle to be used. In the main part of this book we pulled the triangle forward from its original Old Testament use, in order to apply it to miracles in the Gospels. Then we expanded to miracles in Acts. And in our reflections just now we have "pulled it back" into the Old Testament region for which Clowney originally designed it.

Longings for Redemption

Even people who have not read the Bible cannot escape God. According to Romans 1:18–23 they know God. But this kind of inescapable knowledge does not save them. Rather, it condemns them.

In spite of knowing God, they flee from him and worship idols, which are substitutes for God.

People also experience the fact that the world as a whole and their own lives in particular are not as they should be. They have longings for redemption. So they admire heroes in their history. Or they invent fictional stories with hero figures who redeem others from oppression. These stories outside the Bible do not have any special authority. Only the stories in the Bible have divine authorization. Their inclusion in the canon of Scripture implies that they have a definite role in the overall story of redemption, leading from creation to fall to redemption in Christ to consummation in the new heaven and new earth.

By contrast, the stories of heroes outside the Bible have a human origin. But even these stories show some of the pattern of redemption, because the human longing for redemption cannot be completely suppressed. The stories may be twisted by false and counterfeit religious ideas and hopes. And yet some resemblance to the real story in Christ can still be found. These stories can therefore serve as points of contact to raise questions and stimulate discussion with non-Christians. The stories raise the question about how redemptive reality is to be found. We know from Scripture that it is to be found in Christ.[4]

Heroes

For example, is Superman a kind of Christ figure? Not everything corresponds, because Superman only appears to be human—Christ is actually human. But Superman comes from another world and has miracle-working powers.

Is ET a Christ figure? Is Obi-Wan Kenobi of *Star Wars* fame? None of the heroic figures in fiction or nonfiction offers a thorough analogy. But we may ask ourselves why people are attracted to hero figures, and why they want to see movies with redemptive plots. Their longing raises the question; Christ's work offers the fundamental answer.

---

[4] Poythress, *In the Beginning Was the Word*, 195–208, 217–218.

Small Redemptive Plots

We know that the redemption Christ achieved is comprehensive. In its effects it extends to every human ill and every human need and every human sin—even to death itself. And it serves in addition as the foundation for the renewal of the cosmos itself (Rom. 8:19–21). If its effects extend so broadly and deeply, they extend into every individual Christian life and into every human institution. In chapter 8 we looked at specific applications, to Joe who is bored in washing dishes, to Sue who has to discipline her son, to Dave who has failed his chemistry test, and to Jane who hopes to embark on an exciting romance. The particularity of these cases, and many more that we have experienced or could imagine, illustrate the relevance of Christ and what he has achieved.

These cases and others also illustrate the relevance and pervasiveness of redemptive plots. Christ works through the Holy Spirit in Joe's life and in Sue's. As Joe takes to heart what Christ has done, Christ works to carry Joe beyond his boredom. Joe begins to find meaning in serving Christ while washing dishes. As Christ works in Sue's life, she may experience victory in her struggle with selfish anger and laziness. She moves from suffering and struggle into a partial resolution. Sue finds spiritual strength in Christ to repent of evil, selfish motives and to move forward with godly discipline. Her son Tim may grow in grace if he experiences not only regret over the consequences of his sin, but forgiveness in Christ that leads to gratitude and genuine desire to serve God in the future. Obedience under trial leads to reward. That sequence is an instance of a redemptive plot, broadly speaking. God promises a reward to his saints: "from the Lord you will receive the inheritance as your reward" (Col. 3:24).

But we need distinctions: there is a distinction between sanctified obedience and legalistic obedience. Legalistic obedience out of pride and selfish desire for temporal reward can sometimes lead to a *temporary* reward. But the underlying motives are twisted. Even in twisted form, however, they still reflect the original untwisted plot. Legalistic obedience would not be attractive unless it counterfeited true service to God in Christ.

We also need to recognize that failures as well as successes come to us in this life. We may fail again and again to follow God's way. For this failure the answer is forgiveness, obtained on the basis of Christ's obedience. Forgiveness for disobedience is not as excellent a way as a reward for genuine obedience. But it still offers us one form of redemptive plot.

Finally, we need to recognize the downward, tragic plots that take place in human lives—our own lives and the lives of others. Disobedience and folly lead to disasters. I am using the label "tragic plot" quite broadly for any human experience that ends in seeming disaster. There is plenty of disaster. Some of it comes to a person as an immediate consequence of his or her own sin. Some of it comes to victims because other people sin against them. Some of it comes because we live in a fallen world, affected in mysterious and untraceable ways by the fall of Adam. For those who belong to Christ, even suffering has a positive meaning in the end. We are called to "share his sufferings" (Phil. 3:10). We do not know the meaning of each event, and sometimes we may be in agony like Job. Yet it remains true, even when we cannot see it, that "for those who love God all things work together for good, for those who are called according to his purpose" (Rom. 8:28).

The power of Christ's redemption comes to Christians in their suffering, even when they cannot figure it out and when they cannot see how. For Christian believers, suffering does lead in the end to glory, just as it did in the life and death and resurrection of Christ. So each of us who belongs to Christ is constantly living redemptive plots, some seemingly very small, others larger.

The Judgmental Plot

And non-Christians? They receive sunshine and rain and other benefits of common grace:

> For he makes his sun rise on the evil and on the good, and sends rain on the just and on the unjust. (Matt. 5:45)

> For he did good by giving you rains from heaven and fruitful seasons, satisfying your hearts with food and gladness. (Acts 14:17)

Non-Christians experience dim forms of redemptive plots when they receive common grace. But the presence of common grace does not mean that they are saved. If they remain in their lost state, the overall plot of their lives is tragic in the end. An anti-redemptive plot does exist, as it were the mirror image of the redemptive plot. It is the plot we see in Adam and his disobedience.

The situation of blessing in the garden of Eden was disrupted by Adam's sin. And then the disruption spread like a cancer until it resulted in death. This foundational sequence with Adam affected all his descendants. They are all subject to death (Genesis 5). They all experience in their own lives the continued tragedy of sin. The existence of the anti-redemptive plot is why God sent Christ into the world. His redemption is the only way to undo the anti-redemption of sin.

Using Analogies with the Plot of Redemption

Thus, we should recognize analogies between the central meaning of redemption in Christ and the particular experiences of redemption in our lives. We should recognize as well the existence of tragic stories, with destructive endings. As we recognize these analogies, we are better able to live lives in union with Christ, who is our Redeemer. We better appreciate how our lives should rely on his victory and be energized by his presence.

The recognition of analogies does not put our own experiences on the same level with Scripture. Christ's work is unique, and is the foundation for every application of redemption throughout history. Scripture is unique, because it is God's own word. In Scripture, and not elsewhere, we receive a divinely authoritative explanation and interpretation of the meaning of redemption.

Precisely when we understand the uniqueness of Christ's work and the uniqueness of Scripture, we can also begin to understand the relevance of Christ's work to our lives and the implications of

Scripture for our lives. Christ's work and Scripture are supremely relevant precisely because they are unique and foundational. God, not man, has designed Christ's work and Scripture to have implications for everyday lives.

Within the lives of unbelievers we can also recognize dim analogies to the biblical patterns of redemption and judgment. Unbelievers and believers are not alike. There is a vast difference between being lost and being saved. But unbelievers are part of this lost world and participate in common-grace blessings of God. In doing so, they themselves live lives containing both happy endings and tragedies. When we recognize this fact, and when we see God's providential control even in the lives of unbelievers, we put ourselves in a position to explain better the relevance of the gospel to their lives.

We should try to understand our lives in the light of God's instruction in Scripture. In this task, the whole Bible is useful (2 Tim. 3:16–17). The usefulness of Scripture includes the miracles of Jesus in the Gospels. In one dimension, they point forward to the central accomplishment of redemption, the death and resurrection of Christ. In another dimension, they offer links not only backwards to the Old Testament and forward to the book of Acts, but forward to the life of each person now living. Our lives display plots. These plots have analogies with the miracles recorded in the Bible. Our lives are not on the same level as Scripture: Scripture is breathed out by God, and has his authority, while our lives work out under God's providential control. But Scripture *applies* to our lives, and to smaller plots within our lives.

May the God of glory show the glory of Christ through the miracles that he himself has presented to us in the Gospels. May he show us the glory of Christ in his crucifixion and resurrection. Through union with Christ, may God work out the application of redemption in our lives, and cause us to praise and glorify God for his mercy, his majesty, his wisdom, and his promise of eternal life. Through Christ may we experience the new life in the Holy Spirit now, and then eternal life in his presence in the new heaven and the new earth.

Bibliography

Blomberg, Craig. *The Historical Reliability of John's Gospel: Issues and Commentary.* Downers Grove, IL: InterVarsity Press, 2002.

———. *The Historical Reliability of the Gospels.* 2nd ed. Downers Grove, IL: InterVarsity Press, 2007.

Bruce, F. F. *The New Testament Documents: Are They Reliable?* Grand Rapids, MI: Eerdmans, 2003.

Carson, D. A. *The Gospel according to John.* Leicester, England: Inter-Varsity; Grand Rapids, MI: Eerdmans, 1991.

———. "Matthew." In *The Expositor's Bible Commentary.* Vol. 9. Rev. ed. Edited by Tremper Longman III and David E. Garland. Grand Rapids, MI: Zondervan, 2010.

Clowney, Edmund P. *Preaching and Biblical Theology.* Grand Rapids, MI: Eerdmans, 1961.

Collins, C. John. *The God of Miracles: An Exegetical Examination of God's Action in the World.* Wheaton, IL: Crossway, 2000.

Fant, Gene C., Jr. *God as Author: A Biblical Approach to Narrative.* Nashville: B&H, 2010.

Frame, John M. *The Doctrine of the Word of God.* Phillipsburg, NJ: Presbyterian & Reformed, 2010.

France, R. T. *The Gospel of Matthew.* Grand Rapids, MI/Cambridge, UK: Eerdmans, 2007.

Keener, Craig S. *Miracles: The Credibility of the New Testament Accounts.* 2 vols. Grand Rapids, MI: Baker, 2011.

Köstenberger, Andreas J. *John.* Grand Rapids, MI: Baker, 2004.

Leithart, Peter J. *Deep Exegesis: The Mystery of Reading Scripture.* Waco, TX: Baylor University Press, 2009.

Metzger, Bruce M. *A Textual Commentary on the Greek New Testament.* 2nd ed. London/New York: United Bible Societies, 1994.

Murray, John. *Redemption Accomplished and Applied.* Grand Rapids, MI: Eerdmans, 1955.

———. "The Attestation of Scripture." In *The Infallible Word: A Symposium by the Members of the Faculty of Westminster Theological Seminary.* Edited by N. B. Stonehouse and Paul Woolley. Philadelphia: Presbyterian & Reformed, 1946. Pages 1–54.

Osborne, Grant R. *Matthew.* Zondervan Exegetical Commentary on the New Testament. Grand Rapids, MI: Zondervan, 2010.

Phillips, Richard D. *Mighty to Save: Discovering God's Grace in the Miracles of Jesus.* Phillipsburg, NJ: Presbyterian & Reformed, 2001.

Poythress, Vern S. *God-Centered Biblical Interpretation.* Phillipsburg, NJ: Presbyterian & Reformed, 1999.

———. *In the Beginning Was the Word: Language—A God-Centered Approach.* Wheaton, IL: Crossway, 2009.

———. *Inerrancy and Worldview: Answering Modern Challenges to the Bible.* Wheaton, IL: Crossway, 2012.

———. *Inerrancy and the Gospels: A God-Centered Approach to the Challenges of Harmonization.* Wheaton, IL: Crossway, 2012.

———. "Overview of the Bible: A Survey of the History of Salvation." In *The ESV Study Bible.* Wheaton, IL: Crossway, 2008. Pages 23–26. http://www.frame-poythress.org/overview-of-the-bible-a-survey-of-the-history-of-salvation/, accessed July 3, 2014.

———. *Reading the Word of God in the Presence of God: A Handbook for Biblical Interpretation.* Wheaton, IL: Crossway, forthcoming.

———. *Redeeming Science: A God-Centered Approach.* Wheaton, IL: Crossway, 2006.

Stonehouse, N. B., and Paul Woolley, eds. *The Infallible Word: A Symposium by the Members of the Faculty of Westminster Theological Seminary.* Philadelphia: Presbyterian & Reformed, 1967.

Trench, Richard Chenevix. *Notes on the Miracles of Our Lord.* 13th ed. London: Kegan Paul, Trench, & Co., 1886 (also many other editions).

General Index

Abraham, and the sacrifice of Isaac, 106n1
Acts, book of: analogies in, 248; historical reliability of, 21; the Holy Spirit in, 248; on the participation of both Gentiles and Jews in the benefits of Jesus's work on the cross, 124; spread of the gospel in, 77
Adam: as head of the human race, 97n1; sin of, 255
adoption, as sons of God, 41, 108, 112, 216
analogies: analogy between the kingdom of God and the kingdom of this world, 214; in the book of Acts, 248; in the Gospels, 247–248; redemptive analogies, 29–30, 83; using analogies with the plot of redemption, 255–256
anti-redemptive plots, 255. *See also* redemptive plots
application, of Scripture: and connections to didactic passages, 242; examples of specific applications, 83–92; and the Holy Spirit, 244; illustrations of the threefold pattern of application, 60–63; the importance of application, 63–64; kinds of application, 59, 59 (figure); kinds of application to the church, 60 (figure); the threefold pattern of application (the miracle, Jesus's resurrection, the application now), 57–60; the two steps of application, 58, 59 (figure)

baptism, 55–56, 57, 84, 110, 234; the Great Commission formula for, 108, 235
blindness and sight, symbolic use of in the Old Testament to stand for unbelief and faith, 156
Blomberg, Craig, 21n4, 137n2
Bruce, F. F., 21n4

calming a storm, 131; application of, 134–135, 242; Clowney's triangle for, 134 (figure); the significance of power in, 132; the symbolism of water in, 132–133
Carson, D. A., 106n1, 114, 198, 202, 224
church, the, application of redemption to as a corporate body, 60 (figure)

church, the, as a community, 190; application of, 190; Clowney's triangle for the communal dimension of the church, 191 (figure)
cleansing a leper, 119; and analogies in the Gospels, 247–248; application of, 91, 122, 240–241; Clowney's triangle for, 122 (figure); and Jesus's identification with sin, 120; and the leper's showing himself to the priest, 121–122; and the role of faith, 121; the significance of leprosy, 119–120
Clowney, Edmund P., 65, 65n2
Clowney's triangle, 65–68, 251; addition of application to, 67–68, 68n4; for animal sacrifice, 67 (figure); for animal sacrifice, with application, 68 (figure); for the baptism of Jesus, 110 (figure); for the calming of the storm, 134 (figure); for the cleansing of a leper, 122 (figure); for the coin in the fish's mouth, 216 (figure); for the communal dimension of the church, 191 (figure); for the cursing of the fig tree, 227 (figure); for the deliverance of the Gadarene demoniacs, 141 (figure); for the feeding of the 5,000 (John 6), 68–70, 69 (figure); for the feeding of the 5,000 (John 6), with application, 70, 70 (figure); for the feeding of the 5,000 (Matthew 14), 181 (figure); for the healing of the centurion's servant, 126 (figure); for the healing of the man born blind, 71, 71 (figure); for the healing of the man born blind, with application, 71–72, 72 (figure); for the healing of the man with a withered hand, 169 (figure); for the healing of the paralytic, 146 (figure); for the healing of Peter's mother-in-law, 129 (figure); for the healing of two blind men, 157 (figure); for the healing of two blind men at Jericho, 221 (figure); for the healing of the woman with the flow of blood, 153 (figure); for Jesus's triumph over Satan, 178 (figure); for justice and compassionate healing, 173 (figure); for many healings, 116 (figure); for the miracles of the Twelve,

miracles of the Twelve, 166 (figure); the
Twelve's miracles as pointing forward
to Jesus's death and resurrection, 166;
the Twelve's miracles as signs of the
kingdom of God, 165
Jesus, death and resurrection of, 20, 37–39,
38 (figure), 40, 57, 74, 99, 116, 125,
128, 133, 140, 163, 177, 187, 206,
226, 231–232; the close tie of the raising of Lazarus with, 37–38; as an event
with universal relevance, 239; as the
foundation for all benefits from God,
86; as the great miracle, 39 (figure); and
Jesus as the "firstfruits," 38; and Jesus's
reference to Jonah, 132–133; relationship of to the Great Commission, 232;
significance of, 232–235; as a unique
event, 239; as an unrepeatable event,
239. *See also* Jesus, resurrection of, Old
Testament anticipations and foreshadowings of
Jesus, earthly ministry of: and the bringing
of the light of redemptive revelation,
77; as characterized by the fellowship
between the Father and the Son, 107;
and the empowering of the Holy Spirit,
105–106; focus of on the Jewish nation,
194; and the giving of new spiritual
life to people, 99; and the provision of
spiritual food through his teaching, his
miracles, and his very presence, 74; the
unified character and goal of, 47–48
Jesus, resurrection of, New Testament
anticipations and foreshadowings of.
See raising of Jairus's daughter; raising
of Lazarus
Jesus, resurrection of, Old Testament anticipations and foreshadowings of: Daniel,
234; Elijah's raising of the widow of
Zarephath's son, 234; Elisha's raising
of the Shunammite's son, 234; Enoch,
233; the Israelites' coming out of bondage in Egypt and crossing the Red Sea,
234; Jonah, 46, 132–133, 234; Noah,
233–234
Jesus, transfiguration of, 203; application
of, 207; Clowney's triangle for, 206
(figure); link of to Jesus's glorification,
204; miraculous elements involved in,
203, 204; and Moses and Elijah, 205,
206; significance of, 204–205; and the
voice from heaven, 204–205
John, Gospel of: explicit instruction in about
the significance of some of the main

miracles in, 95; purpose of, 21; on the
purpose of Jesus's miracles, 26
John, Gospel of, miracles in. *See* feeding of
the 5,000 (John 6); healing of the man
born blind; healing of the official's son;
healing of the sick man at the Sheep
Gate; Jesus, death and resurrection of;
raising of Lazarus; walking on water
(John 6); water turned into wine
John the Baptist, 44; John's baptism as a
baptism "for repentance," 108; John's
baptism as baptism with water, 44; message of warning and call to repentance
of, 225; resistance of to the idea of
baptizing Jesus, 108; as the terminus of
the whole Old Testament order, 44
Jonah, metaphorical death-and-resurrection
experience of, 46, 132–133, 234; Jesus's
reference to, 132–133

Keener, Craig S., 18
kingdom of God, 249; authority as a characteristic of, 125; and comprehensive
deliverance, 115; conflict of with the
kingdom of Satan, 139, 176–178; as the
exercise of God's saving power in climactic form, 48–49; feast of, 43; God's
kingdom purpose of salvation as starting with the Jews and then extending
to the Gentiles, 194; growth of through
the activities of networks of people in
communities, 190; Jesus's instruction to
"seek first the kingdom of God," 215;
unity of, 48–49
kingdom of heaven. *See* kingdom of God
kingdom of Satan, 139; conflict of with the
kingdom of God, 139, 176–178; defeat
of, 139–140

Leithart Peter J., 79n2
leprosy, 119–120; passages in the Mosaic law
regarding leprosy, 121; and the process
of going to the priest, 121; role of in
Old Testament ceremonial law, 120;
touching a leper, 120
light: the creation of light, 79; Jesus as the
light of the world (John 9), 35–36, 36
(figure), 38–39, 51; New Testament
theme of, 156; Old Testament theme
of, 79
Luke, Gospel of, Luke's reason for writing
it, 20–21

marriage, depiction of in the Old Testament,
90

materialistic worldview, 19; influence of science on, 19

Matthew, Gospel of, miracles in. *See* calming a storm; cleansing a leper; coin in the fish's mouth; cursing the fig tree; deliverance of the Gadarene demoniacs; feeding of the 4,000; feeding of the 5,000 (Matthew 14); healing of a blind and mute man; healing of a boy with a demon; healing of the centurion's servant; healing of the man with a withered hand; healing of a mute demoniac; healing of a paralytic; healing of Peter's mother-in-law; healing of two blind men; healing of two blind men at Jericho; healing of the woman with a flow of blood; Jesus, baptism of; Jesus, death and resurrection of; miracles of healing, of Jesus; raising of Jairus's daughter; Syrophoenician woman, the; virgin birth, the; walking on water (Matthew 14)

Matthew, Gospel of, organization of to highlight Jesus's teaching, 162; the five conspicuous blocks of text that contain Jesus's teaching, 205

Messiah, the, 28; Jesus as the Messiah, 27, 28–29, 101, 163

Metzger, Bruce M., 137n2

Mighty to Save: Discovering God's Grace in the Miracles of Jesus (Phillips), 30, 51, 247

Miracles: The Credibility of the New Testament Accounts (Keener), 18

miracles, of Jesus: as acts of God, 18; applications of, 91–92, 240–244, 243 (figure); and context, 70; credibility of in the Gospels, 20–21, 23; as the depiction and embodiment of redemption, 57–59; did Jesus's miracles really happen? 18–19; and the glory of God, 58, 61; multiple thematic connections of, 80–81; plot structure of (transition from trouble to resolution), 50–51; as pointing to Jesus's death and resurrection, 46, 46 (figure), 91, 95, 232; purpose of, 26; raising of the widow's son in Nain, 26; reiteration of a miracle as reinforcement of a point, 220; relevance of to particular situations, 240–243; as signs, 26–27, 42, 68; as signs of the kingdom of God, 95; universal relevance of, 239–240. *See also* miracles, of Jesus, the pattern of redemption in; miracles, of Jesus, significance of; miracles of

exorcism, of Jesus; miracles of healing, of Jesus; *specific miracles in the Gospel of John and the Gospel of Matthew*

miracles, of Jesus, the pattern of redemption in: and the inner unity of redemption, 49–51; and the narrative form of the Gospels, leading to climax, 49; and the unified character and goal of Jesus's ministry, 47–48; and the unity of the kingdom of God, 48–49

miracles, of Jesus, significance of, 26–27, 27 (figure), 29–30: the miracles show deity, 27, 27–28; the miracles show that Jesus is the Messiah, 27, 28–29; the miracles show Jesus as a prophet in his humanity, 27, 28

miracles, in the Old Testament, 27–28, 248–251; Elijah's provision for the widow of Zarephath, 69, 77; Elijah's raising of the widow of Zarephath's son, 25, 38, 234; Elisha's bringing relief from famine, 69, 77; Elisha's healing of Naaman the Syrian, 79–80; Elisha's multiplication of bread, 69, 77, 180; Elisha's raising of the Shunammite's son, 25, 38, 234; in the exodus from Egypt, 248–249; the flood, 249; Jonah, 46, 132–133, 234; Joseph's deliverance of people from the famine in Egypt, 77; the manna from heaven, 34, 69, 76–77, 180; as works of divine power, 28

miracles of exorcism, of Jesus, 160, 210. *See also specific miracles of exorcism*

miracles of healing, of Jesus: accomplishment of on the Sabbath, 40, 168; application of, 116–117, 164–165, 172, 199; Clowney's triangle for justice and compassionate healing, 173 (figure); Clowney's triangle for many healings, 116 (figure); Clowney's triangle for shepherding and harvesting, 165 (figure); Clowney's triangle for wonder at healings, 199 (figure); and harvesting imagery, 163–164; link of with the servant passages in Isaiah, 114, 172; redemptive plots of, 115–116; and the response of wonder, 198–199; and shepherding imagery, 162–163, 164; significance of, 113–115, 162–164, 198–199, 217–218; summaries of the many healings, 113, 113–114, 161–162, 171, 189–190, 197–198, 217–218; and the theme of faith, 210. *See also specific miracles of healing*

139; defeat of, 139–140, 177–178; involvement of in the deaths of Job's sons and daughters, 131n1; as the "strong man" Jesus binds, 139–140. *See also* demons; kingdom of Satan

science: God as the foundation for, 20; influence of on the modern materialistic worldview, 19; scientific law, 20

Scripture, 256; as God-breathed, 256; usefulness of, 256. *See also* application, of Scripture

sea, the: God's mastery of, 186; as a symbol for the final abyss of hell, 141; as a symbol for what is unmasterable, 186

semeion (Greek: sign), 26

servant passages in Isaiah, 28–29, 114, 172

shepherding imagery, 162–163, 164, 180; God as the true shepherd, 162; Israel's false shepherds, 162; Jesus as a shepherd, 162, 180

sickness, 40

sin, 141; the fundamental disorder of as symbolically represented by the subordinate disorders of demon possession and sickness, 114; as a kind of spiritual paralysis, 125, 144; as moral and spiritual rebellion against God, 97n1

Son of David, 156, 219–220

Son of God: Jesus as, 98, 101, 106–108, 112, 131, 145, 185–188, 214, 216; in the Old Testament, 185–186; Peter's confession of Jesus as the "Christ, the Son of the living God," 185

Son of Man, 168; Jesus as, 168

sōzō (Greek: to save, to make well), 152

Stonehouse, N. B., 21n5

suffering, 254; as an emblem or sign of the results of sin, 125–126, 144

Syrophoenician woman, the, 193–194; application of, 195; Clowney's triangle for, 195 (figure); significance of, 194

temple curtain, rending of, 236

tragic plots, 254, 255

tree of life: connection with the river of life, 75; in the consummation, 75; in the garden of Eden, 76

Trinity, the, 107–108; and harmony as a fundamental indication that there is an eternal relationship of Father to Son in the Trinity, 107, 107n2; and the unity of one God in three persons, 108

types and typology, 65, 249, 251. *See also* Clowney's triangle

unbelievers, 256

uncleanness: communication of by touch, 120, 150; of dead bodies, 150; of lepers, 119–120; pigs as a symbol of, 140; as a symbol of sin and death, 120, 140–141; of women with a discharge of blood, 150, 152

unfruitfulness, 224, 225, 226

union with Christ, 128, 255; and redemption, 55

virgin birth, the, 96, 107; application of, 103–104; broader implications of, 98–101; circles of meaning for, 100 (figure); Clowney's triangle for, 98 (figure); Clowney's triangle for, with application, 101 (figure); and the dream given to Joseph, 102; as fulfillment of promises and patterns in the Old Testament, 99–100; as fulfillment of the prophecy in Isaiah 7:14, 96, 99; the miracles surrounding the wise men, 102–103; significance of, 96–98; smaller miracles taking place in connection with the virgin birth, 101–103

walking on water (John 6), 45–46

walking on water (Matthew 14), 183–184; application of, 188; and the challenge to have faith, 187; Clowney's triangle for, 188 (figure); connection of to Jesus's crucifixion and resurrection, 187; and inaugurated and consummated eschatology, 46; and Jesus as the Son of God, 185–188; Old Testament background of, 186; significance of, 184–185; threats that Jesus overcomes, 184. *See also* Peter, and Jesus's walking on water

water: as symbolic of death, 46, 132–133; symbolic association of with Jewish rites of purification, 43–44

water turned into wine, 42–45; application of, 91, 240; and inaugurated and consummated eschatology, 45

Woolley, Paul, 21n5

Scripture Index

ALSO AVAILABLE FROM VERN S. POYTHRESS

Redeeming Mathematics   Poy

REDEEMING PHILOSOPHY   POYTH

REDEEMING SOCIOLOGY   PO

IN THE BEGINNING
WAS THE WORD   POYTHI

INERRANCY AND WORLDVIEW   POYTHR

INERRANCY AND THE GOSPELS   POYTHR

CHANCE AND THE SOVEREIGNTY OF GOD   PO

Redeeming SCIENCE   POY

Logic | Poythress

Printed in the USA
CPSIA information can be obtained
at www.ICGtesting.com
LVHW041738140823
755219LV00035B/576

9 781433 546075